To my taste testers: my amazing husband, Greg, and my two sweet children, Reagan and Skyler

100
Delicious
No-Fuss Meals
for Busy
People

The Easy
5-INGREDIENT
SLOW COOKER
Cookbook

Karen Bellessa Petersen

Photography by Melina Hammer

ROCKRIDGE
PRESS

CONTENTS

INTRODUCTION

Dinnertime can sometimes be stressful for all of us. Busy schedules, cranky kids, and other challenges can test our patience when it comes to putting a good dinner on the table. Well, I'm here to help you. I develop delicious recipes for homemade, family-friendly slow cooker dinners, and in this book, I share my recipes with you.

In 2009, I was a stay-at-home mom with two small children. I'll never forget trying to make dinner with a kid (or two) hanging off my leg. I thought, "There has to be a better way!" Fortunately, I discovered the slow cooker and fell in love with it.

The slow cooker allowed me to get dinner started in the middle of the morning while my kids were napping. In fact, I loved the freedom the slow cooker gave me so much that I decided to use it to cook dinner for 365 days straight and to write a blog (365DaysOfCrockpot.com) to share the recipes with my readers. Writing the blog provided accountability, which helped me fulfill my goal, and I learned how to cook along the way! Now, many years later, my kids are involved in sports and other activities and they still keep me busy. They aren't hanging off my leg at five o'clock anymore, but they need

me to drive them here and there or help with homework. Lucky for me, I still use the slow cooker, and I love the support it provides to busy people. I truly appreciate how my family can eat when we're ready because the slow cooker is waiting for us on warm until we get home.

I've created over a thousand slow cooker recipes over the past eight years. I have also discovered all sorts of handy tips and tricks for the slow cooker that I will share with you in this book. For example, I've learned what cuts of meat to use, why you can't add dairy to a recipe at the beginning, why you shouldn't lift the lid of the slow cooker for the first 2 hours, and how to intensify flavors. I've also learned from my blog readers that they mostly want super simple and fast recipes they can get going in the morning.

I want to help you make delicious, highly nutritious food in the least amount of preparation time possible. I've kept my recipes short and sweet by limiting the primary ingredients to 5 items in each. Whether you are a working professional who is tired when you get home, a busy parent with a very hungry family, a college student who needs to study instead of cook, or an empty-nester working on your golf game, this book can help you. So let's get cooking!

1

SLOW
& EASY

Whether you're a working professional, a stay-at-home parent, a student, or a retiree, weeknight dinners just seem to be a challenge to get on the table, don't they? We're all busy rushing around at work or at home getting errands done, homework accomplished, household duties looked after, and appointments kept. And the hour that we should be preparing dinner—from 5 to 6 p.m.—seems to be the busiest! Some moms of young toddlers call it the witching hour because their young children seem to turn into crazy monsters then. That's why I'm a huge fan of the slow cooker.

The slow cooker can help you get a home-cooked meal on the table without any stress. My favorite recipes for the slow cooker have very few ingredients and minimal preparation time. You just put the ingredients in the slow cooker in the morning and let this incredible appliance slowly cook your meal all day long. Then when you're ready to eat, your dinner will be waiting for you!

In this opening chapter, I will discuss the benefits of using the slow cooker and I'll give you some of my best slow cooker tips and tricks. I'll also preview what's ahead in the recipes and tell you how to stock your pantry so you'll be ready to start cooking. And I'll share some ideas on how to round out a meal.

THE ALMIGHTY SLOW COOKER

I just love how easy slow cookers are to use. Usually they have only a few temperature settings, and there are no burners to be afraid of if you are a first-time cook. The slow cooker is an appliance that should be in every household. Here are some essential things to know about the slow cooker:

* The slow cooker uses an indirect heat source and doesn't scorch. You don't need to stir the food as you would if it were on a stove-top burner. The slow cooker uses moist heat to cook food, so don't lift the lid—every time you do, you are releasing the steam that is surrounding and cooking the food.

* Make sure to taste your food before serving. Because moisture does not evaporate in the slow cooker, flavors and spices can mellow and dissipate as time goes by. I often add seasonings right before serving slow-cooked food.

* Slow cookers typically have just three settings: warm, low, and high, so they are easy to work with. All slow cookers cook differently. I have ten different slow cookers, and some cook faster than others. So you will want to get to know your slow cooker.

* There are several different sizes of slow cookers. In this book all recipes were written using a 6-quart oval slow cooker, which seems to be the most popular size.

* If you are often away from home for several hours at a time, I suggest that you invest in a slow cooker with a timer on it. When you set the timer for the cooking time in the recipe, the slow cooker will switch to warm when the food is done, and will stay on warm (safely for up to 4 hours) until you can get home.

* Don't reheat slow cooker leftovers in the slow cooker, because bacteria can grow in the time it takes for the food to reach a safe temperature.

* I've learned the hard way not to place a hot slow cooker insert on a cold countertop or in a cold sink. The ceramic insert can crack if it is exposed to abrupt temperature shifts.

* To remove stains in your slow cooker insert, simply fill it with water, add 1 cup of white vinegar, cover, and cook on high for 2 hours.

PLAN-AHEAD TIME-SAVERS

The recipes in this book are easy to make and require very little preparation time. There are a few steps you can take to make them even easier:

- Read the entire recipe and collect all the ingredients (and any equipment needed) before you begin cooking. This will save you from the frustration of finding out you don't actually have potatoes in your pantry as you thought.

- Put frozen foods in the refrigerator to thaw the day before you want to cook them. I make a menu plan for the week, which helps me remember when to defrost frozen meats or other foods.

- Onions add lots of flavor to savory dishes. Dehydrated onions (also called onion flakes or dried minced onion) save a lot of time at the cutting board. About ¼ cup dried onion is equal to 1 cup chopped fresh onion.

- If you're constantly in a rush in the morning, prepare some or all parts of the recipe the night before. Store the food in an airtight container in the refrigerator, and then pop it into the slow cooker in the morning, set the timer, and off you go.

- Many soups and stews start off with a flavor base of aromatic vegetables, namely carrots, celery, and onion, called *mirepoix*. To avoid peeling and chopping, I often use a package of frozen "mirepoix-style blend," which you can find in the frozen vegetable aisle of many supermarkets.

SLOW COOKER OR CROCK-POT?

The term *slow cooker* is the generic name for an appliance that uses heating elements all around the insert, which bring food up to safe temperatures. Crock-Pot is the Rival corporation's registered trademark for its slow cookers. All Crock-Pots are slow cookers, but not all slow cookers are Crock-Pots. Other popular slow cooker brands include All-Clad, Cuisinart, and Hamilton Beach.

When you're shopping for a slow cooker, please keep in mind that there are appliances on the market referred to as slow cookers that have their heating element only on the bottom. Don't buy one of these to use for the recipes in this book. Appliances with heating elements only on the bottom heat food more slowly than those with heating elements all around the insert. Experts do not recommend cooking large cuts of meat in this type of slow cooker (although it works for soups and stews). So when purchasing your slow cooker, please make sure it is a true one—with heating elements all around the insert.

EASY, ESSENTIAL PREP

There are two kinds of slow cooker prep: essential, like peeling and chopping, and optional, like sautéing, roasting, and browning. This book is designed to help home cooks get their dinners together as fast as possible, so the recipes do not include any optional kinds of prep. However, if you have a little extra time and want to develop more depth of flavor, here are some guidelines:

* Sautéing certain ingredients will give the dish a more balanced, mellow aroma and a slightly sweeter, smoother flavor. When aromatics are heated in fat—like butter or oil—at the beginning of a recipe, the heated fat helps these ingredients release aromas and impart deep flavors into the dish as it is being cooked. Aromatics include onions, garlic, carrots, celery, and ginger.

* Roasting involves cooking food in the oven in an uncovered pan. Dry, hot air surrounds the food, cooking it evenly on all sides. I like to prepare a side dish of roasted vegetables to go with a meat dish that has been slow cooked; three of my favorite roasted veggies are beets, potatoes, and butternut squash.

* There are no rules about browning meat before placing it in the slow cooker. For recipes that contain many spicy aromatic ingredients, you may achieve a tasty dish without browning. But if you do have the time, I suggest browning the following meats for enhanced flavor: ground turkey, ground beef, ground sausage, pork loin, and eye of round roast.

EASY 5-INGREDIENT RECIPE MANIFESTO

Here's what to expect from the recipes you'll find in this cookbook:

5 INGREDIENTS: As you flip through this book and peruse some of the recipes, you will probably notice that some of the recipes have more than 5 ingredients listed. That's because each recipe contains only 5 primary ingredients (which are highlighted in yellow), plus some pantry staples and simple spices. These pantry staples and spices are listed in the sections that follow.

ONE-POT MEALS: The recipes in this book are intended to be complete meals. Sometimes you may want to serve a side dish (like a salad or a steamed vegetable), but usually the dish is enough for a meal on its own. These recipes will help you get a meal on the table effortlessly.

DELICIOUSNESS: I've tested all these recipes on my family and friends, and they all ate them happily. I'm sure you'll find many recipes in the book that will become family favorites.

15 MINUTES OF PREP: The recipes found in this book will require no more than 15 minutes of prep time and no mandatory precooking requirements. If you want, you'll be able to throw everything into the slow cooker in the morning, leave, and come home later to a nutritious, delicious cooked meal.

THE RECIPES COOK FOR 8+ HOURS: I know that many of you are hardworking professionals who simply want dinner "done" by the time you get home from work. So at least half of the recipes I developed for the book require 8 hours of cooking time. Some recipes require less time; you may want to make these on the weekends or consider investing in a slow cooker with a timer and automatic warming function.

ZERO PROCESSED FOODS: The recipes in this book don't contain ingredients like canned soup, dry soup mix, packaged seasoning mixes, or other highly processed, artificially flavored ingredients. I love recipes that use ingredients such as dried beans cooked from scratch and fresh vegetables. Some recipes in the book use real-food convenience products such as canned beans, canned tomatoes, tomato sauce, tomato paste, canned broth, frozen vegetables, salsa, dried spices, and other similar items. If you want to eat more healthfully, when a recipe calls for any of these ingredients, you can always choose an organic and/or low-sodium version of the item.

MIX OF RECIPES: I've tried to include a wide variety of recipes in this book that incorporate plenty of your favorite comfort foods but also include a range of international dishes.

SLOW COOKER TEMPERATURES

Slow cookers typically have three settings: low, high, and warm. Most slow cookers set on low reach temperatures ranging from 185° to 200°F, depending on the individual slow cooker. On high, they reach temperatures between 250° and 300°F. I own several different slow cookers and they all cook differently. So when you are getting to know your slow cooker, regard the recipe cooking times as guidelines but not hard truths. I used a 6-quart oval slow cooker to test the recipes in this book. If you're finding that all your recipes are getting overdone, then you may want to reduce the recommended cooking times given here.

RECIPE TIPS AND LABELS

Every recipe in this book includes a tip or label to address common questions and concerns:

SUPER EASY: This tip will help you make the recipe even easier and faster. For example, you could use frozen diced onions instead of dicing the onions yourself.

TASTY TIP: I'll share with you an optional step to enhance the flavor of the dish, if you wish to try it. For example, I may suggest sautéing the onions before adding them to the stew.

INGREDIENT TIP: If there's a hint I know about prepping a particular ingredient, I'll share it with you—for example, how to clean leeks or how to remove the skin from chicken thighs.

SIMPLE SWAP: I'll share easy substitutes that you can make for certain ingredients. For example, using frozen corn kernels rather than having to cook ears of corn and cut off the kernels.

BIG 8 ALLERGEN FREE: This label indicates that a recipe is free of any of the Big 8 Allergens: dairy, eggs, fish, crustacean shellfish, peanuts, tree nuts, wheat, or soybeans.

ALLERGY TIP: If a recipe includes one of the Big 8 Allergens, I'll recommend an ingredient substitution if possible. (But if the recipe is, say, an egg casserole, where the main ingredient is eggs, which can't be substituted in a satisfactory way, you'll need to forgo making that recipe.)

SET AND FORGET: This label indicates a recipe that requires 8 or more hours of cooking time and no prep at the end.

THE SUPER SIMPLE PANTRY

The basic staple ingredients you should have in your refrigerator or pantry to make the recipes in this book are listed below. These staples are not part of the 5 primary ingredients, because they are considered general kitchen supplies.

BROTH: Most of the recipes that call for broth use chicken broth. But a few recipes call for beef broth or vegetable broth. Broth adds a deep flavor that can't be duplicated by simply adding water.

BUTTER: There's no substitute for butter! Sometimes a couple of tablespoons of butter can make all the difference in a recipe. I use unsalted butter, so I can control the amount of salt going into my recipes.

CORNSTARCH: Slow cooker recipes can end up runny because no evaporation occurs over the long cooking time. A little cornstarch can thicken up a sauce in just minutes.

FLOUR: Just as cornstarch is used to thicken several of the recipes, so is flour. I use all-purpose flour, but you can use whole-wheat flour if you prefer.

MILK: I use milk in several recipes to add a touch of creaminess. You can use 1 percent, 2 percent, or whole milk, whichever you prefer.

SUGAR: Not many of my recipes call for sugar or brown sugar, but sometimes just a tablespoon of brown sugar can make a barbecue recipe go from meh to memorable.

OIL: Several of the recipes in this book call for olive oil or canola oil. Keep your oil in a glass or glazed ceramic container in a cool, dark cupboard. I also use nonstick cooking spray.

THE SUPER SIMPLE SPICE RACK

I'll always remember my husband's uncle saying, "Spices are 1 percent of the volume of ingredients in a recipe but account for how it turns out 99 percent of the time." Food always turns out better when it's properly seasoned.

Something as simple as salt and freshly ground black pepper can turn a bland, tasteless dish into a fantastic one. I'll never forget going to a local restaurant and ordering a curry soup. It tasted very mediocre. When I took the leftovers home and added a touch of salt and freshly ground black pepper, the soup was outstanding.

The following dried herbs and spices should be kept in a dark cupboard, ready for use. Herbs and spices listed in recipes don't count toward the 5 primary ingredients in my recipes.

DRIED BASIL: If a kitchen has only a few herbs in the cupboard, basil will likely be one of them. Its fragrant essence combines well with rosemary and thyme in dishes containing meat, fish, vegetables, cheese, and eggs.

DRIED OREGANO: Whether fresh or dried, oregano is one of the foundations of Greek and Italian cuisine because of its ability to draw out the best of any ingredient it's blended with, particularly in tomato-based dishes.

DRIED THYME: Fresh or dried thyme leaves and flowers lend a sprightly essence to casseroles, soups, stews, and sautéed vegetables.

BAY LEAF: Bay leaves are unlike the other herbs in the spice cabinet. While we eat most herbs, these aromatic leaves are best used whole and then removed from the pot before serving. The leaf itself doesn't taste like much, but when steeped in a warm broth or sauce, the dish becomes infused with fragrant flavor.

GROUND CAYENNE PEPPER: Used in both savory and sweet recipes, just a pinch of this powerful red powder is all you need to punch up the heat.

CHILI POWDER: Chili powder is a blend of the herbs and spices most commonly found in Latin American cooking. The base ingredients are usually ground ancho chile, paprika, ground cumin, and dried Mexican oregano.

GROUND CUMIN: Cumin (whole or ground) is one of those spices that's essential for any spice cupboard. Just 1 teaspoon adds a hint of smokiness. Use more and your dish will be infused with sweet, earthy flavors.

GROUND CINNAMON: You are probably familiar with cinnamon, which is used in treats like apple pie and cinnamon rolls. But cinnamon is a versatile spice that is sometimes used in savory dishes as well.

GROUND GINGER: Ground ginger has a warm, spicy bite, is a little bit sweet, and is not as strongly flavored as fresh ginger.

GARLIC POWDER: Garlic powder is ground dehydrated garlic.

ONION POWDER: Onion powder is ground dehydrated onion.

SMOKED PAPRIKA: Smoked paprika is made from smoked red peppers. It can be used to add authentic smoky flavor to dishes.

GET WITH THE PROGRAM

If you don't own a programmable slow cooker, you may want to buy a socket timer. A socket timer allows the slow cooker to automatically turn off at a certain time. Simply plug the timer into an outlet and then plug the slow cooker into the timer. Then you can set the timer according to the recipe directions. For example, if you want the food to cook for only 7 hours but you'll be away for 8 hours, set the timer to shut off the slow cooker 1 hour before you return. But keep in mind that you don't want any meal containing meat to sit in the slow cooker for more than 2 hours, because this can cause bacteria to grow and cause foodborne illness. But if you're cooking something like steel-cut oatmeal, you can set the socket timer to start the slow cooker hours after you leave (or go to bed) for a delayed start time.

ROUNDING OUT SLOW COOKER MEALS

The slow cooker dinner recipes in this book are one-pot meals. With some of them, though, you may want to add a side dish. Here are a few suggestions for rounding out your dinner:

BREAD OR ROLLS: A good-quality whole-grain bread is a perfect dipper for soup or stew. You can easily pick up a loaf of fresh French bread or quickly thaw previously purchased bread stored in your freezer.

BROCCOLI: One of my standard side dishes is broccoli. I either steam a package of frozen broccoli in the microwave, or roast fresh broccoli for 15 minutes in the oven with a bit of olive oil, lemon, and grated Parmesan cheese.

BROWN RICE: Several of the recipes in this book are meats with sauces of some sort. Brown rice is perfect to provide a whole grain with the meat and to soak up the sauce. Brown rice takes a long time to cook on the stove (about an hour), so I make a big batch all at one time and freeze 1-cup portions in resealable plastic bags in the freezer. Then when I need some rice, all I have to do is reheat it in the microwave.

CORN BREAD: There's nothing like a hunk of cornbread to go with your chili or stew. You can get fancy and search for a jalapeño corn bread recipe or sour cream corn bread recipe or just use the recipe on the cornmeal package.

GREEN SALAD: I always keep a big bag or tub of mixed greens, such as washed and dried spinach, chard, and kale, in our refrigerator. These greens are ready for making an easy salad with some of our favorite salad dressings, like balsamic vinaigrette or Italian dressing. I also keep grape or cherry tomatoes handy to slice up and serve on the salad.

RAW VEGGIES: Once a week I cut up fresh vegetables, like celery, carrots, bell peppers, and cucumbers, and keep them in an airtight container in my refrigerator. Then I prepare an easy Greek yogurt dip by mixing plain yogurt with dried herbs, garlic powder, salt, and pepper. These veggies and dip are a perfect side dish for a meaty meal.

FREEZING SLOW-COOKED FOOD

Depending on how many people you are serving, some of the recipes in this book may provide you with leftovers. Freezing leftovers is a great option for upcoming busy nights or an easy way to bring lunch to work next week. I like to freeze my leftovers in resealable plastic freezer bags and lay them flat in my freezer so they'll stack nicely. Some meals freeze better than others. Here are some tips:

- Don't freeze recipes that are cream-based. They will separate, and the texture will be off when reheated.

- Don't freeze potatoes unless they're hash browns. Potatoes take on a grainy texture if frozen and then reheated.

- Don't freeze cooked pasta. The flavor will be diminished and the texture will be mushy.

- Make sure the food you are freezing has had a chance to cool down before you freeze it. Cover it tightly with foil in a casserole dish or place it in a resealable plastic freezer bag.

- Defrost and serve frozen leftovers within 3 months.

BREAKFAST

Crustless Spinach Quiche

SERVES 6 • PREP TIME: 10 MINUTES
COOK TIME: 5 HOURS

Nonstick cooking spray

4 large eggs

1 cup half-and-half

1 cup shredded sharp Cheddar cheese

3 cups fresh baby spinach leaves

2 cups cubed ham

½ teaspoon salt

¼ teaspoon freshly ground
black pepper

I like to make crustless quiche for a healthier, gluten-free alternative to traditional quiche. It's a natural for brunch, or sometimes I make it as a "breakfast for dinner." I like to use fresh spinach in the recipe to give it a pop of color, some extra nutrition, and a bit more texture.

1 Spray the slow cooker with nonstick cooking spray.

2 In a large bowl, beat the eggs. Add the half-and-half, Cheddar cheese, spinach, ham, salt, and pepper and stir to combine. Pour the mixture into the slow cooker.

3 Cover and cook on low for 5 hours or on high for 3 hours.

4 Turn off the slow cooker and let it sit for 15 minutes before serving.

SIMPLE SWAP You can use frozen spinach instead of fresh spinach leaves. Empty a box of frozen spinach into a colander. Run warm water over the spinach until it's warm. Then use a clean towel or paper towels to press down on the spinach and release as much water as possible.

ALLERGY TIP If you are allergic to dairy, use coconut milk in place of the half-and-half and a vegan cheese as a substitute for the Cheddar.

PER SERVING Calories: 381; Total Fat: 27g; Saturated Fat: 14g; Cholesterol: 277mg; Sodium: 1,459mg; Total Carbohydrates: 7g; Fiber: 1g; Protein: 27g

Egg, Hash Brown, and Sausage Breakfast Casserole

SERVES 4 TO 6 • PREP TIME: 10 MINUTES
COOK TIME: 4 HOURS

Nonstick cooking spray

6 large eggs

½ cup milk

Salt

Freshly ground black pepper

8 ounces cooked sausage links, cut into bite-size pieces

1 (1-pound) package frozen hash browns

½ cup salsa or picante sauce

1 cup shredded sharp Cheddar cheese

You can prepare this recipe the night before and put it in the refrigerator until you're ready to cook it in the morning. We like this dish for Christmas morning. Since we wake up so early on Christmas, I just put this recipe in the slow cooker and cook it on high for 2 hours instead of on low for 4 hours.

1 Spray the slow cooker with nonstick cooking spray.

2 In a large bowl, whisk together the eggs and milk and season with salt and pepper. Pour the mixture into the slow cooker. Add the sausage, hash browns, salsa, and cheese and stir.

3 Cover and cook on low for 4 hours, or until the potatoes are cooked through and the eggs are set.

4 Turn off the slow cooker and let it sit for 15 minutes before serving.

SUPER EASY If you have the time, you can use ground breakfast sausage instead of sausage links. Just brown the sausage in a skillet on the stove top and drain off the fat before adding the sausage to the slow cooker. You can also substitute crumbled cooked bacon for the sausage, if you prefer.

ALLERGY TIP If you're allergic to dairy, you can substitute vegan versions of the milk and cheese.

PER SERVING Calories: 674; Total Fat: 50g; Saturated Fat: 19g; Cholesterol: 346mg; Sodium: 1,013mg; Total Carbohydrates: 37g; Fiber: 3g; Protein: 29g

Spinach-Mushroom Frittata

SERVES 4 • PREP TIME: 10 MINUTES
COOK TIME: 3 HOURS

Nonstick cooking spray

6 large eggs

1 cup sliced mushrooms

1 cup fresh baby spinach leaves

⅓ cup minced scallions

1 teaspoon garlic powder

Salt

Freshly ground black pepper

1 cup shredded sharp Cheddar cheese

You may not know that you can put an oven-safe dish inside your slow cooker insert—I like to use this method when I want to ensure my food will cook evenly and not stick to the sides of the insert.

1 Make sure you use an oven-safe baking dish that fits inside your slow cooker insert. Spray the baking dish with nonstick cooking spray.

2 In a large bowl, beat the eggs. Add the mushrooms, spinach, scallions, and garlic powder and stir to combine. Season with salt and pepper. Pour the egg mixture into the baking dish. Sprinkle with the cheese. Place the dish in the slow cooker.

3 Cover and cook on low for 3 hours, or until set.

4 Turn off the slow cooker and let it sit for 15 minutes before serving.

SIMPLE SWAP If you'd rather use fresh garlic, substitute 2 minced garlic cloves. You can also use jarred minced garlic, which you can find in the produce section of your grocery store.

ALLERGY TIP If you are allergic to dairy, substitute a vegan cheese for the Cheddar.

PER SERVING Calories: 233; Total Fat: 17g; Saturated Fat: 8g; Cholesterol: 309mg; Sodium: 328mg; Total Carbohydrates: 3g; Fiber: 1g; Protein: 18g

Egg and Cheese Bake

SERVES 6 • PREP TIME: 15 MINUTES
COOK TIME: 4 HOURS

Nonstick cooking spray

3 cups French bread cubes, toasted

1½ cups shredded sharp Cheddar cheese

5 slices cooked bacon, crumbled

6 large eggs

3 cups milk

¾ teaspoon salt

¼ teaspoon freshly ground black pepper

This breakfast casserole can be put together the night before, covered, and refrigerated. Simply pop the insert into the slow cooker in the morning, and cook on low for 4 hours or on high for 2 hours. This delicious dish is a perfect choice for brunch.

1 Spray the slow cooker with nonstick cooking spray. Add the bread cubes, cheese, and bacon and stir to combine.

2 In a medium bowl, whisk together the eggs, milk, salt, and pepper. Pour over the bread mixture.

3 Cover and cook on low for 4 hours.

4 Turn off the slow cooker and let it sit for 15 minutes before serving.

SUPER EASY There's nothing like freshly cooked crispy bacon, but sometimes it can be challenging to cook, especially when you're short on time. For those days, I purchase a package of already cooked all-natural bacon slices, warm up 5 slices in the microwave per the instructions, and crumble them. I find the precooked bacon in my grocery store with the packaged meats.

INGREDIENT TIP Be sure to use sharp Cheddar cheese. It imparts the best cheesy flavor to the dish.

PER SERVING Calories: 569; Total Fat: 36g; Saturated Fat: 17g; Cholesterol: 365mg; Sodium: 1,620mg; Total Carbohydrates: 24g; Fiber: 1g; Protein: 37g

Blueberry-Coconut Quinoa

SERVES 4 • PREP TIME: 10 MINUTES
COOK TIME: 3 HOURS

BIG 8 ALLERGEN FREE

¾ cup quinoa, rinsed and drained

¼ cup shredded unsweetened coconut

1 tablespoon honey

1 (13.5-ounce) can coconut milk

2 cups fresh blueberries

This breakfast quinoa uses coconut milk, shredded coconut, and blueberries, but you can use a different type of berry in place of blueberries. If you live in the Pacific Northwest, blackberries in late summer would be an excellent option.

1 Put the rinsed quinoa in the slow cooker. Sprinkle the coconut over the top and then drizzle with the honey.

2 Open the can of coconut milk. Stir until smooth and even in consistency. Pour over the quinoa.

3 Cover and cook on low for 3 hours.

4 Stir the quinoa, then scoop it into four serving bowls. Top each bowl with blueberries and serve.

SIMPLE SWAP If fresh blueberries are not in season or aren't available, you can easily substitute frozen blueberries, which are available year-round.

PER SERVING Calories: 468; Total Fat: 33g; Saturated Fat: 27g; Cholesterol: 0mg; Sodium: 21mg; Total Carbohydrates: 43g; Fiber: 7g; Protein: 8g

Apple-Cinnamon Oatmeal

SERVES 4 • PREP TIME: 10 MINUTES
COOK TIME: 4 HOURS

1 cup steel-cut oats

1 tablespoon unsalted butter, melted

4 cups water

¼ cup brown sugar

1 teaspoon ground cinnamon

½ teaspoon salt

1 Granny Smith apple, peeled, cored, and chopped

½ cup milk

I love the chewy texture of steel-cut oats. For this slow cooker recipe, make sure you use regular steel-cut oats and not the quick-cooking kind so the cook time is accurate. If you're the only one in your house who likes steel-cut oats (like me), you can easily reheat leftovers for a fast breakfast option when you're in a rush.

1 Combine the steel-cut oats and butter in the slow cooker. Stir until the oats are coated with the butter. Add the water, brown sugar, cinnamon, and salt.

2 Cover and cook on low for 4 hours.

3 Stir the chopped apple into the oatmeal. Scoop into four serving bowls and serve with a splash of milk.

TASTY TIP Instead of using water to cook the oatmeal, use apple juice. If you use this method, leave out the ¼ cup brown sugar or else the oatmeal may be too sweet. Just top each serving with 1 teaspoon of brown sugar to sweeten.

ALLERGY TIP If you're allergic to dairy, use melted coconut oil instead of the butter.

PER SERVING Calories: 143; Total Fat: 4g; Saturated Fat: 2g; Cholesterol: 10mg; Sodium: 329mg; Total Carbohydrates: 25g; Fiber: 3g; Protein: 3g

Baked Oatmeal

SERVES 4 TO 6 • PREP TIME: 10 MINUTES
COOK TIME: 3 HOURS

⅓ cup canola oil

1 large egg

¾ cup milk

2 cups quick-cooking oats

½ cup sugar

1½ teaspoons baking powder

½ teaspoon salt

This breakfast treat tastes so good you may think you're biting into a warm-from-the-oven oatmeal cookie. It's wonderful served with milk or topped with blueberries or bananas.

1 Pour the canola oil into the slow cooker and tilt to coat the bottom and sides thoroughly.

2 In a medium bowl, beat the egg. Add the milk, oats, sugar, baking powder, and salt and mix well. Pour the mixture into the slow cooker.

3 Cover and cook on low for 3 hours, or until tender. Serve.

ALLERGY TIP If you're allergic to eggs, use an egg substitute. If you're allergic to dairy, use almond milk or soy milk.

PER SERVING Calories: 348; Total Fat: 21g; Saturated Fat: 2g; Cholesterol: 50mg; Sodium: 332mg; Total Carbohydrates: 37g; Fiber: 1g; Protein: 5g

French Toast Casserole

SERVES 8 • PREP TIME: 10 MINUTES
(PLUS REFRIGERATION TIME)
COOK TIME: 4 HOURS

6 large eggs

2 cups milk

1 teaspoon vanilla extract

1½ teaspoons ground
cinnamon, divided

**1 (1-pound) loaf French bread
(preferably stale), cubed**

4 tablespoons (½ stick) unsalted
butter, at room temperature

½ cup brown sugar

You can get as creative with toppings on this French toast casserole as you want. Serve it with whipped cream, cut-up bananas or other fruit, pure maple syrup, or a fancy syrup like buttermilk caramel.

1 Whisk together the eggs, milk, vanilla, and ½ teaspoon of cinnamon in the slow cooker. Submerge the bread cubes in the mixture; if necessary, put a plate on top to keep the bread submerged. Cover and refrigerate for at least 4 hours or up to overnight.

2 In a small bowl, mix the butter, brown sugar, and remaining 1 teaspoon of cinnamon. Scatter the topping over the bread mixture.

3 Cover and cook on low for 4 hours.

4 Turn off the slow cooker and let it sit for 15 minutes before serving.

SIMPLE SWAP You can use challah or brioche in place of French bread in this recipe, if you prefer. The bread soaks up the egg mixture more readily if it is somewhat stale, so you can buy day-old bread for this dish.

PER SERVING Calories: 403; Total Fat: 12g; Saturated Fat: 6g; Cholesterol: 160mg; Sodium: 645mg; Total Carbohydrates: 58g; Fiber: 2g; Protein: 16g

Chapter

3

SOUP

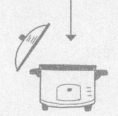

Beef and Barley Soup

SERVES 6 TO 8 • PREP TIME: 15 MINUTES
COOK TIME: 8 HOURS

BIG 8 ALLERGEN FREE
SET AND FORGET

3 cups chicken broth

3 cups beef broth

1 tablespoon tomato paste

2 cups frozen mirepoix

1½ pounds beef chuck roast, trimmed of excess fat and cut into bite-size pieces

⅔ cup pearl barley (not quick-cooking)

8 ounces sliced mushrooms

1 bay leaf

1 teaspoon onion powder

1 teaspoon garlic powder

¾ teaspoon dried thyme

1 teaspoon salt, plus more for seasoning

½ teaspoon freshly ground black pepper, plus more for seasoning

On a cold winter day, this soup is like comfort in a bowl. If some members of your family don't care for mushrooms, you can leave them out. I like to buy barley in the bulk section of the grocery store.

1 Combine all the ingredients in the slow cooker and stir.

2 Cover and cook on low for 8 hours.

3 Discard the bay leaf. Season with additional salt and pepper, if needed. Ladle into bowls and serve.

SUPER EASY Instead of trimming and cubing a chuck roast, you can simply buy chunks of beef stew meat instead. Beef stew meat is usually sold in 1-pound packages. To reduce prep time even further, you can buy the mushrooms already washed and sliced.

PER SERVING Calories: 298; Total Fat: 9g; Saturated Fat: 3g; Cholesterol: 70mg; Sodium: 1,249mg; Total Carbohydrates: 21g; Fiber: 5g; Protein: 31g

Tomato Soup

SERVES 6 • PREP TIME: 10 MINUTES
COOK TIME: 8 HOURS

SET AND FORGET

1 cup frozen mirepoix

⅓ cup all-purpose flour

1 (28-ounce) can crushed tomatoes

1 (6-ounce) can tomato paste

1 tablespoon dried basil

1 teaspoon dried oregano

1 teaspoon salt, plus
more for seasoning

4 cups chicken or vegetable broth

1 bay leaf

1 cup milk, warmed

2 tablespoons unsalted butter

Freshly ground black pepper

⅔ cup grated Parmesan cheese

On a cold day, there's nothing better than a bowl of tomato soup with grilled cheese sandwiches. I use crushed tomatoes in this recipe because I like how they give the soup body and texture. For creaminess, I use milk and a little bit of butter. The result is a lightly creamy, bright tomato soup.

1 Combine the mirepoix, flour, crushed tomatoes, tomato paste, basil, oregano, and salt in the slow cooker. Use a whisk to stir the flour into the tomatoes to incorporate. Add the broth and stir. Add the bay leaf.

2 Cover and cook on low for 8 hours.

3 Discard the bay leaf. Stir in the warm milk and butter until the butter is melted. Season with additional salt and pepper, if desired.

4 Ladle the soup into bowls, top each serving with Parmesan cheese, and serve.

SIMPLE SWAP Don't have crushed tomatoes on hand? Just use a can of diced tomatoes and pulse them a few times with an immersion blender.

ALLERGY TIP If you have trouble digesting dairy, leave out the milk and butter, and substitute soy milk mixed with melted dairy-free soy margarine. Opt for a vegan cheese instead of Parmesan.

PER SERVING Calories: 200; Total Fat: 8g; Saturated Fat: 5g; Cholesterol: 22mg; Sodium: 955mg; Total Carbohydrates: 25g; Fiber: 6g; Protein: 11g

Black Bean Soup

SERVES 6 • PREP TIME: 10 MINUTES
COOK TIME: 8 HOURS

BIG 8 ALLERGEN FREE
SET AND FORGET

8 ounces dried black beans, picked over and rinsed

3½ cups water

1 smoked ham hock, rinsed

1 bay leaf

1 teaspoon dried oregano

1 teaspoon ground cumin

1 teaspoon garlic powder

1 teaspoon salt, plus more for seasoning

Juice of 1 lime

1 (8-ounce) can tomato sauce

Freshly ground black pepper

Chopped fresh cilantro, for garnish

Dried beans and the slow cooker just go together, don't they? I especially love black beans since I don't have to remember to soak them before adding them to the slow cooker. Just don't add any acidic ingredients (like lime juice or tomato sauce) before the beans are done cooking or they'll never get tender.

1 Combine the black beans, water, ham hock, bay leaf, oregano, cumin, garlic powder, and salt in the slow cooker.

2 Cover and cook on low for 8 hours, or until the beans are tender.

3 Discard the bay leaf. Stir in the lime juice and tomato sauce. Season with additional salt and pepper, if desired.

4 Ladle into soup bowls and garnish with cilantro.

INGREDIENT TIP Dried beans need to be washed and sorted before using because they often have dust and little rocks in them.

SIMPLE SWAP If you can't find ham hocks at the grocery store, you can substitute 4 ounces of any of the following: chopped salted pork, chopped smoked bacon, chopped smoked ham, smoked sausage, or a ham bone.

PER SERVING Calories: 237; Total Fat: 7g; Saturated Fat: 3g; Cholesterol: 43mg; Sodium: 632mg; Total Carbohydrates: 23g; Fiber: 6g; Protein: 21g

French Onion Soup

SERVES 4 • PREP TIME: 15 MINUTES
COOK TIME: 8 HOURS

SET AND FORGET

**3 small yellow onions,
cut into thin rings**

¼ cup olive oil or canola oil

Pinch salt

Pinch freshly ground black pepper

Pinch sugar

2 (13.5-ounce) cans beef consommé

½ cup water

**4 slices crusty bread (French
bread or a baguette works well)**

1⅓ cups shredded Gruyère cheese

French onion soup is a classic recipe, but it can take a lot of hands-on time if made on the stove top. That's why I love the slow cooker! It is a perfect tool for caramelizing onions. I pair this soup with a simple salad tossed with balsamic vinaigrette.

1 Put the onions in the slow cooker. Add the olive oil, salt, pepper, and sugar and stir until the onions are coated.

2 Cover and cook on low for 8 hours, or until the onions are soft and caramelized.

3 Pour in the consommé and water and turn the slow cooker to high. Cook until warmed through, about 10 minutes.

4 Position the top oven rack about 6 inches below the broiler. Turn on the broiler.

5 Ladle the soup into four oven-safe bowls and place them on a rimmed baking sheet. Place a piece of bread on top of each serving of soup. Sprinkle ⅓ cup of Gruyère cheese on top of each piece of bread.

6 Broil for 1 to 2 minutes, or until the cheese is melted and starts to brown. Serve immediately.

SIMPLE SWAP If you have a hard time finding Gruyère cheese, you can use Swiss cheese instead.

ALLERGY TIP If you're allergic to dairy, you'll want to omit the cheese. If you're allergic to wheat, you can use a wheat-free bread or forgo the bread altogether.

PER SERVING Calories: 384; Total Fat: 24g; Saturated Fat: 9g; Cholesterol: 33mg; Sodium: 966mg; Total Carbohydrates: 28g; Fiber: 3g; Protein: 17g

Lemony Lentil and Chicken Soup

SERVES 6 • PREP TIME: 15 MINUTES
COOK TIME: 6 HOURS

1 medium yellow onion,
very thinly sliced

1 cup brown lentils

1 pound boneless, skinless chicken
thighs, trimmed of excess fat

1 teaspoon garlic powder

5 cups chicken broth

3 large egg yolks

¼ cup fresh lemon juice

Salt

Freshly ground black pepper

This brightly flavored soup is based on the Greek classic *avgolemono* soup, which translates as "egg-lemon." The creaminess comes from the egg yolks that are added at the end of the cooking time. Serve this light, healthy soup with some crusty bread.

1 Combine the onion, lentils, chicken, garlic powder, and chicken broth in the slow cooker.

2 Cover and cook on low for 6 hours.

3 Transfer the chicken to a cutting board. Shred the chicken with two forks and return it to the slow cooker.

4 In a small bowl, whisk together the egg yolks and lemon juice. Stir the mixture into the slow cooker. Season with salt and pepper and serve.

SIMPLE SWAP If you don't have brown lentils on hand, you can use green lentils instead. I can usually find lentils next to the dried beans at the grocery store. Sometimes they are also found in the bulk aisle.

ALLERGY TIP If you're allergic to eggs, leave out the egg yolks. They provide a creaminess to the soup, so you can add ½ cup of half-and-half or Greek yogurt instead.

PER SERVING Calories: 277; Total Fat: 8g; Saturated Fat: 2g; Cholesterol: 158mg; Sodium: 736mg; Total Carbohydrates: 23g; Fiber: 10g; Protein: 29g

Mexican Corn Chowder

SERVES 6 TO 8 • PREP TIME: 15 MINUTES
COOK TIME: 8 HOURS

**1 (16-ounce) package frozen
sweet white corn kernels**

1 teaspoon salt, plus
more for seasoning

½ teaspoon freshly ground black
pepper, plus more for seasoning

½ teaspoon ground cumin

4 cups chicken broth

½ cup picante sauce

**4 medium russet potatoes, peeled
(about 1½ pounds total)**

**4 bone-in, skinless chicken
thighs, trimmed of excess fat**

2 to 3 tablespoons fresh lime juice

The star of this soup is the bright lime juice.
It enhances all the Mexican flavors and brings
them together. Half of the potatoes are smashed
to create a thicker consistency rather than using
flour or cream.

1 Put the corn in the slow cooker. Sprinkle in the salt,
pepper, and cumin. Pour in the broth and the picante
sauce. Submerge the potatoes in the liquid. Nestle the
chicken thighs in among the potatoes.

2 Cover and cook on low for 8 hours.

3 Transfer the chicken to a cutting board. The meat
should practically fall off the bones. Discard the cartilage
and bones. Shred the chicken with two forks and return
it to the slow cooker.

4 Transfer the potatoes to the cutting board. Smash two
of the potatoes with a fork and stir into the slow cooker.
Cut the remaining two potatoes into cubes. Gently stir the
cubed potatoes and lime juice into the slow cooker. Season
with additional salt and pepper, if desired. Ladle the soup
into bowls and serve.

SIMPLE SWAP Instead of using bone-in chicken thighs, you can
use boneless chicken thighs.

RECIPE TIP To give the soup more color, texture, or additional
flavors, feel free to garnish each bowl with chopped bell pepper,
bacon, cilantro, or black pepper before serving.

PER SERVING Calories: 250; Total Fat: 4g; Saturated Fat: 1g;
Cholesterol: 63mg; Sodium: 1,087mg; Total Carbohydrates: 31g;
Fiber: 5g; Protein: 22g

Broccoli Cheddar Soup

SERVES 5 • PREP TIME: 10 MINUTES
COOK TIME: 8 HOURS

SET AND FORGET

2 cups chicken broth

1 pound Yukon Gold potatoes, peeled

1 medium yellow onion, diced

2 scallions, minced

1 teaspoon garlic powder

¼ teaspoon ground thyme

Salt

Freshly ground black pepper

1 (1-pound) package frozen broccoli florets, thawed and drained

½ cup shredded extra-sharp Cheddar cheese

½ cup milk

1 tablespoon unsalted butter

Usually broccoli Cheddar soups are loaded with cream and cheese, which makes them delicious but not such a healthy choice. This version uses potatoes as the base. Yukon Gold potatoes are cooked until tender and then puréed, giving the soup creaminess and a buttery flavor. Just add a bit of Cheddar cheese and milk to finish it off.

1 Combine the broth, potatoes, onion, scallions, garlic powder, and thyme in the slow cooker. Season with salt and pepper.

2 Cover and cook on low for 8 hours.

3 Carefully transfer the contents of the slow cooker to a blender, in batches if necessary. Purée until smooth, making sure to vent the blender lid for steam. Add three-quarters of the broccoli. Pulse three or four times to get the soup to your desired consistency.

4 Pour the soup back into the slow cooker. Add the Cheddar, milk, butter, and remaining broccoli and stir. Season with additional salt and pepper, if needed.

5 Turn the slow cooker to high and cook for a few minutes, until warmed through. Serve.

SUPER EASY Make this recipe even faster by using an immersion blender to purée the soup in the slow cooker. There will also be less cleanup than if you use your countertop blender.

ALLERGY TIP If you have trouble digesting dairy, you'll want to omit the milk, butter, and use a vegan cheese in this recipe.

PER SERVING Calories: 194; Total Fat: 8g; Saturated Fat: 5g; Cholesterol: 20mg; Sodium: 431mg; Total Carbohydrates: 24g; Fiber: 5g; Protein: 10g

Chicken Enchilada Soup

SERVES 6 • PREP TIME: 10 MINUTES
COOK TIME: 8 HOURS

**BIG 8 ALLERGEN FREE
SET AND FORGET**

1 cup chicken broth

1½ cups picante sauce

1 (15-ounce) can enchilada sauce

**1 (14.5-ounce) can black
beans, rinsed and drained**

**1½ pounds boneless, skinless chicken
thighs, trimmed of excess fat**

1 teaspoon ground cumin

1 (14.5-ounce) can refried beans

Sour cream, for topping (optional)

This enchilada soup is super easy to start cooking in the morning and will warm you up on those cold winter days! It's ultra creamy without using dairy, thanks to the addition of a can of refried beans. Make it spicy with a hot enchilada sauce, or for those weaklings (like me), just use mild.

1 Combine the broth, picante sauce, enchilada sauce, black beans, chicken, and cumin in the slow cooker.

2 Cover and cook on low for 8 hours.

3 Transfer the chicken to a cutting board. It should be very tender. Shred the chicken with two forks.

4 Add the refried beans to the slow cooker and stir until blended. Gently stir in the shredded chicken. Ladle the soup into bowls, top each serving with a dollop of sour cream (if using), and serve.

SIMPLE SWAP You can easily swap out the black beans for a different type of bean such as pinto beans, chickpeas, or navy beans. Or, if you're not a fan of beans, you can leave them out and add 2 cups of frozen sweet corn. If you don't want to use refried beans to add thickness and creaminess to the soup, you can stir in 2 cups of sour cream instead.

PER SERVING Calories: 273; Total Fat: 8g; Saturated Fat: 2g; Cholesterol: 87mg; Sodium: 1,417mg; Total Carbohydrates: 22g; Fiber: 9g; Protein: 28g

Chicken and Pesto Soup

SERVES 6 • PREP TIME: 15 MINUTES
COOK TIME: 6 HOURS

3½ cups chicken broth

2 carrots, peeled and cut into ¼-inch rounds

2 celery stalks, cut into ¼-inch slices

1 teaspoon dried oregano

1 teaspoon garlic powder

5 boneless, skinless chicken thighs, trimmed of excess fat

½ cup long-grain brown rice

1½ cups milk, at room temperature

½ cup basil pesto

One of my family's favorite foods is pesto sauce. The bright flavors from the basil pesto are perfect with pasta. But have you ever considered adding it to a soup? I love how the flavor (and color) of this soup is brightened by the green pesto sauce.

1 Combine the broth, carrots, celery, oregano, and garlic powder in the slow cooker and stir. Add the chicken and rice and stir.

2 Cover and cook on low for 6 hours, or until the chicken is cooked through and the rice is tender.

3 Transfer the chicken to a cutting board. Shred the chicken with two forks or cut it into small pieces. Return the chicken to the slow cooker. Stir in the milk and pesto.

4 Cover and cook on high for 10 minutes, until warmed through. Ladle into bowls and serve.

SIMPLE SWAP If you can't find boneless, skinless chicken thighs, you can use bone-in chicken thighs. Simply remove the skin before placing them in the slow cooker. Then, after the cooking time is up, remove the chicken and place on a cutting board. The meat should just fall off the bones, and you can discard the bones and use the meat in the soup.

ALLERGY TIP If you have trouble digesting dairy, just leave out the milk or replace it with almond milk. If you're allergic to pine nuts, you'll need to make your own pesto sauce without pine nuts.

PER SERVING Calories: 239; Total Fat: 8g; Saturated Fat: 2g; Cholesterol: 72mg; Sodium: 573mg; Total Carbohydrates: 18g; Fiber: 1g; Protein: 25g

Chicken and Barley Soup

SERVES 6 • PREP TIME: 10 MINUTES
COOKING TIME: 6 HOURS

BIG 8 ALLERGEN FREE

5 boneless, skinless chicken thighs, trimmed of excess fat

½ cup pearl barley (not quick-cooking)

3 cups frozen mirepoix

3½ cups chicken broth

1 (14.5-ounce) can diced tomatoes, undrained

1 tablespoon tomato paste

1 bay leaf

1 teaspoon dried basil

1 teaspoon garlic powder

¾ teaspoon salt, plus more for seasoning

¼ teaspoon freshly ground black pepper, plus more for seasoning

Few things are as satisfying as a bowl of warm soup. I have been making versions of this recipe for years, and I love the chewy barley and chunks of chicken. I like to serve this soup with a side salad and a hunk of crusty bread.

1 Combine all the ingredients in the slow cooker and stir to combine.

2 Cover and cook on low for 6 hours.

3 Discard the bay leaf. Transfer the chicken to a cutting board. Shred the chicken with two forks or cut it into small pieces. Return the chicken to the slow cooker. Season with additional salt and pepper, if desired. Ladle the soup into bowls and serve.

INGREDIENT TIP I almost always use canned tomatoes in my slow cooker recipes because I know that canned tomatoes are packed at the peak of freshness. And although I can't think of anything better than a fresh garden tomato, there's really only a few weeks out of the year that they're available.

PER SERVING Calories: 164; Total Fat: 6g; Saturated Fat: 2g; Cholesterol: 67mg; Sodium: 908mg; Total Carbohydrates: 6g; Fiber: 2g; Protein: 22g

Creamy Cauliflower-Broccoli Soup

SERVES 6 • PREP TIME: 10 MINUTES
COOK TIME: 8 HOURS

SET AND FORGET

2 pounds cauliflower florets

2 scallions, minced

2 cups chicken or vegetable broth

1 teaspoon onion powder

1 teaspoon garlic powder

¼ teaspoon dried thyme

½ teaspoon salt, plus
more for seasoning

¼ teaspoon freshly ground black
pepper, plus more for seasoning

**1 (12-ounce) package
frozen broccoli florets**

**½ cup grated Parmesan cheese,
plus more for optional garnish**

¼ cup heavy cream

This healthy, creamy soup features puréed cauliflower and bright green broccoli florets. There is just a bit of Parmesan cheese and cream in the soup, but that little bit goes a long way for flavor.

1 Combine the cauliflower, scallions, broth, onion powder, garlic powder, thyme, salt, and pepper in the slow cooker.

2 Cover and cook on low for 8 hours.

3 Carefully transfer the contents of the slow cooker to a blender, in batches if necessary. Purée until smooth, making sure to vent the blender lid for steam. Pour the puréed soup back into the slow cooker.

4 Stir in the broccoli, Parmesan cheese, and cream. Cover and cook on high for 10 minutes, or until heated through.

5 Season with additional salt and pepper, if needed. Ladle the soup into bowls and garnish with more Parmesan cheese, if desired.

SUPER EASY I usually buy a head of cauliflower and cut it up into florets. But if you're in a real hurry, you can find a package of fresh cauliflower florets in the produce section of your grocery store. You can also use frozen cauliflower florets for this recipe, but since the frozen cauliflower will add more liquid to the soup, you'll want to reduce the amount of broth to 1½ cups.

ALLERGY TIP If you have trouble digesting dairy, leave out the heavy cream and the Parmesan cheese. If you wish, you can stir in ¼ cup of soy half-and-half.

PER SERVING Calories: 124; Total Fat: 5g; Saturated Fat: 3g; Cholesterol: 14mg; Sodium: 642mg; Total Carbohydrates: 14g; Fiber: 6g; Protein: 10g

Ham and White Bean Soup

SERVES 8 • PREP TIME: 10 MINUTES
(PLUS SOAKING THE BEANS OVERNIGHT)
COOK TIME: 8 HOURS

BIG 8 ALLERGEN FREE
SET AND FORGET

1 pound dried great northern beans, picked over and rinsed

1 tablespoon salt, plus
½ teaspoon, divided

6 cups chicken broth

6 cups water

2 cups cubed ham

2 cups frozen mirepoix

1 teaspoon dried basil

1 teaspoon dried oregano

¼ teaspoon freshly ground black pepper, plus more for seasoning

2 bay leaves

½ teaspoon liquid smoke

I don't make ham very often, but when I do I always look forward to the leftovers. I love making ham and bean soup in the slow cooker with dried beans. My favorite accompaniment for this soup is a classic corn bread.

1 The night before you make the soup, put the beans in a large bowl and add enough water to cover them by 2 inches. Sprinkle in 1 tablespoon of salt. Soak the beans for at least 8 hours.

2 The next day, drain the water and rinse the beans thoroughly. Put the beans in the slow cooker. Add the chicken broth, 6 cups fresh water, ham, mirepoix, basil, oregano, remaining ½ teaspoon of salt, pepper, bay leaves, water, and liquid smoke.

3 Cover and cook on low for 8 hours, or until the beans are tender.

4 Discard the bay leaves. Season with additional salt and pepper, if desired. Ladle into bowls and serve.

SIMPLE SWAP You can substitute dried navy beans, pinto beans, or even kidney beans for the great northern beans. Just make sure to soak the dried beans in salty water overnight so they'll cook up with softer skins.

TASTY TIP If you have a ham bone, throw that into the soup as well for an extra layer of flavor.

PER SERVING Calories: 287; Total Fat: 3g; Saturated Fat: 1g; Cholesterol: 15mg; Sodium: 1,245mg; Total Carbohydrates: 42g; Fiber: 14g; Protein: 24g

Chapter

4

CHILI & STEW

Turkey-Lentil Chili

SERVES 4 • PREP TIME: 10 MINUTES
COOK TIME: 8 HOURS

SET AND FORGET

1 pound ground turkey

2 teaspoons chili powder

1 teaspoon garlic powder

1 teaspoon ground cumin

½ teaspoon freshly ground black pepper

1 cup green or brown lentils

2½ cups water

2 cups mild picante sauce

**1 (4-ounce) can diced
green chiles, drained**

4 tablespoons sour cream

I love this chili because it is so easy to make—and delicious. The picante sauce is a key ingredient because it enhances the flavor. My kids like to crumble corn chips on top of their chili for an extra crunch. If you have time, you could brown the ground turkey before adding it to the slow cooker for extra depth of flavor or garnish it with some chopped chives or scallions.

1 Put the ground turkey in the slow cooker. Using a wooden spoon, break up the turkey.

2 Add the chili powder, garlic powder, cumin, pepper, lentils, water, picante sauce, and chiles.

3 Cover and cook on low for 8 hours.

4 Use a wooden spoon to break up the meat into even smaller pieces. Ladle the chili into bowls and top each serving with 1 tablespoon of sour cream.

SIMPLE SWAP One time when I was making this recipe, I didn't realize I was out of lentils. How can I make lentil chili without lentils? I ended up using barley in its place and it turned out great! I love the chewiness of the barley.

ALLERGY TIP If you are allergic to dairy, leave out the sour cream.

PER SERVING Calories: 403; Total Fat: 6g; Saturated Fat: 2g; Cholesterol: 67mg; Sodium: 1,624mg; Total Carbohydrates: 44g; Fiber: 16g; Protein: 42g

White Chicken Chili

SERVES 4 • PREP TIME: 10 MINUTES
(PLUS SOAKING THE BEANS OVERNIGHT)
COOK TIME: 8 HOURS

**BIG 8 ALLERGEN FREE
SET AND FORGET**

1 cup dried great northern beans, rinsed and picked over

1 tablespoon salt, plus
½ teaspoon, divided

4 cups chicken broth

1 teaspoon garlic powder

1 teaspoon ground cumin

1 teaspoon dried oregano

¼ teaspoon freshly
ground black pepper

1 pound bone-in, skinless chicken thighs, trimmed of excess fat

1½ cups frozen sweet white corn

1½ tablespoons fresh lime juice

Chopped fresh cilantro,
for garnish (optional)

White chicken chili is a favorite among kids and adults alike. One variation that works really well with this recipe is to use leftover cubed turkey after Thanksgiving in place of the chicken thighs. Another variation is to use canned great northern beans instead of dried beans. If you do use canned beans, you will need to cook the soup for only 6 hours and you can reduce the broth to 3 cups.

1 The night before you make the chili, put the dried beans in a large bowl and add enough water to cover them by 2 inches. Sprinkle in 1 tablespoon of salt. Soak the beans for at least 8 hours.

2 The next day, drain the water and rinse the beans thoroughly. Put the beans in the slow cooker. Add the chicken broth, garlic powder, cumin, oregano, remaining ½ teaspoon of salt, pepper, and chicken.

3 Cover and cook on low for 8 hours, or until the beans are tender.

4 Transfer the chicken to a cutting board. Remove the chicken bones and discard. Shred the meat and return it to the slow cooker. Stir in the corn and lime juice.

5 Cover and cook on high for about 10 minutes, or until the corn is heated through. Ladle the chili into bowls and garnish with cilantro (if using).

INGREDIENT TIP I like to use bone-in chicken thighs in my slow cooker because they stay moist and tender, unlike chicken breasts. To remove the skin from a chicken thigh, grasp the skin tightly at the joint end and pull it off in one piece. If necessary, use a sharp knife to cut the skin off. To get a secure hold, you can also grasp the skin with a piece of paper towel. I keep a box of disposable rubber gloves in my kitchen to handle messy meat projects like this.

PER SERVING Calories: 259; Total Fat: 6g; Saturated Fat: 2g; Cholesterol: 53mg; Sodium: 633mg; Total Carbohydrates: 28g; Fiber: 3g; Protein: 26g

Buffalo Chicken Chili

SERVES 6 • PREP TIME: 10 MINUTES
COOKING TIME: 6 HOURS

1½ pounds boneless, skinless chicken thighs, trimmed of excess fat

2 (15-ounce) cans great northern beans, rinsed and drained

1 (14.5-ounce) can diced fire-roasted tomatoes

2 cups chicken broth

¼ to ½ cup buffalo wing sauce

½ teaspoon onion powder

½ teaspoon garlic powder

¼ teaspoon salt

8 ounces cream cheese

Blue cheese crumbles (optional)

This chili can be as spicy or as mild as you like it. I always start with less hot sauce and then add more at the end if I feel it needs more kick. We like to serve this chili with celery sticks.

1 Combine the chicken, beans, tomatoes with their juice, broth, ¼ cup of buffalo wing sauce, onion powder, garlic powder, and salt in the slow cooker.

2 Cover and cook on low for 6 hours.

3 Cut the cream cheese into cubes and stir them into the slow cooker. Transfer the chicken to a cutting board. Shred the chicken with two forks or cut it into small pieces. Return the chicken to the slow cooker.

4 When the cream cheese is melted and incorporated into the chili, ladle the chili into bowls and serve. Top with blue cheese crumbles, if desired.

SIMPLE SWAP   You can substitute navy beans for the great northern beans.

ALLERGY TIP   If you are allergic to dairy, use vegan cream cheese and leave out the blue cheese.

PER SERVING Calories: 322; Total Fat: 19g; Saturated Fat: 10g; Cholesterol: 122mg; Sodium: 939mg; Total Carbohydrates: 11g; Fiber: 3g; Protein: 27g

Pork and Beans Chili

SERVES 6 • PREP TIME: 15 MINUTES
(PLUS SOAKING THE BEANS OVERNIGHT)
COOK TIME: 8 HOURS

**BIG 8 ALLERGY FREE
SET AND FORGET**

**1 pound dried pinto beans,
rinsed and picked over**

1 tablespoon plus salt,
½ teaspoon, divided

4 cups water

2 (8-ounce) cans tomato sauce

2 tablespoons molasses

1 tablespoon Dijon mustard

Freshly ground black pepper

5 slices cooked bacon, crumbled

Your childhood favorite pork and beans can be made at home in your slow cooker with dried beans and lots of crumbled bacon and just a few other pantry staples. This recipe can easily be doubled for a potluck supper.

1 The night before you make the soup, put the dried beans in a large bowl and add enough water to cover them by 2 inches. Sprinkle in 1 tablespoon of salt. Soak the beans for at least 8 hours.

2 The next day, drain the water and rinse the beans thoroughly. Put the beans in the slow cooker. Add 4 cups fresh water.

3 Cover and cook on low for 8 hours, or until the beans are tender.

4 Drain off any extra water. Add the tomato sauce, molasses, mustard, remaining ½ teaspoon of salt, and a few grinds of pepper and stir. Add the crumbled bacon and serve.

SIMPLE SWAP If you don't have any cooked bacon on hand, just cook up 5 slices of bacon until crispy. Place the cooked bacon on a paper towel to absorb the grease, and then crumble the bacon into the chili.

PER SERVING Calories: 387; Total Fat: 8g; Saturated Fat: 2g; Cholesterol: 17mg; Sodium: 1,190mg; Total Carbohydrates: 57g; Fiber: 13g; Protein: 23g

Cincinnati Chili

SERVES 4 TO 6 • PREP TIME: 15 MINUTES
(PLUS SOAKING THE BEANS OVERNIGHT)
COOK TIME: 8 HOURS

Cincinnati chili is a Mediterranean-spiced meat sauce used as a topping for spaghetti. There are many ways to make it, but in this recipe, we're going five-way: spaghetti, chili, shredded cheese, diced onions, and beans.

SET AND FORGET

¾ cup dried kidney beans, rinsed and picked over

3 teaspoons salt, divided

2½ cups water

1 pound lean ground beef

1 tablespoon chili powder

1 teaspoon ground cumin

1 teaspoon ground cinnamon

½ teaspoon garlic powder

½ teaspoon onion powder

¼ teaspoon freshly ground black pepper, plus more for seasoning

2 (8-ounce) cans tomato sauce

Cooked spaghetti, for serving

1 cup shredded Cheddar cheese, for garnish

1 cup chopped red onion, for garnish (optional)

1 The night before you make the chili, put the dried beans in a large bowl and add enough water to cover them by 2 inches. Sprinkle in 2 teaspoons of salt. Soak the beans for at least 8 hours.

2 The next day, drain the water and rinse the beans thoroughly. Put the beans in the slow cooker. Pour in 2½ cups fresh water. Add the ground beef, chili powder, cumin, cinnamon, garlic powder, onion powder, remaining 1 teaspoon of salt, and the pepper and stir to combine.

3 Cover and cook on low for 8 hours, or until the beans are tender.

4 Stir in the tomato sauce. Season with additional salt and pepper, if desired.

5 To serve, pile some spaghetti on each plate and ladle the chili over the top. Garnish with Cheddar cheese and chopped red onion, if desired.

TASTY TIP If you want to add extra flavor, you can brown the ground beef. An option that I find helpful is to buy ground beef in bulk when it's on sale. I brown it immediately when I get home from the grocery store. I store the meat in 1-pound portions in resealable plastic bags in the freezer. Whenever I need a pound of ground beef, I have it on hand.

ALLERGY TIP If you're allergic to dairy, simply leave out the Cheddar cheese or substitute a vegan cheese.

PER SERVING Calories: 599; Total Fat: 38g; Saturated Fat: 17g; Cholesterol: 115mg; Sodium: 1,450mg; Total Carbohydrates: 30g; Fiber: 8g; Protein: 35g

Chunky Chili con Carne

SERVES 4 • PREP TIME: 15 MINUTES
COOK TIME: 8 HOURS

BIG 8 ALLERGEN FREE
SET AND FORGET

1 pound beef chuck roast, trimmed of fat and cut into bite-size pieces

1½ teaspoons chili powder

1 teaspoon ground cumin

1 teaspoon garlic powder

½ teaspoon salt, plus
more for seasoning

¼ teaspoon freshly ground black pepper, plus more for seasoning

1 medium yellow onion, finely diced

2 (14.5-ounce) cans petite diced tomatoes

2 tablespoons tomato paste

¾ cup water

1 (15-ounce) can kidney beans, rinsed and drained

A great chili is perfect for get-together and watch-the-game events. This beefy chili contains kidney beans because I'm one of those people who think chili needs beans. But if you're a meat purist, you can leave out the beans. If you do, add some diced green pepper and scallions to serve on top of the chili.

1 Put the beef in the slow cooker. Sprinkle on the chili powder, cumin, garlic powder, salt, and pepper. Stir to combine.

2 Add the onion, tomatoes with their juice, tomato paste, water, and beans. Stir to combine.

3 Cover and cook on low for 8 hours, or until the beef is tender.

4 Stir the chili and season with additional salt and pepper, if desired. Ladle into bowls and serve.

TASTY TIP To enhance the flavor of this dish, you can brown the beef with the seasonings in a skillet. Just heat 2 teaspoons of olive oil over medium-high heat. Swirl the pan to coat with oil. Add the beef and sprinkle with the seasonings. Sauté the beef for 5 minutes, or until evenly browned. Transfer the meat to the slow cooker and follow the instructions to make the chili.

PER SERVING Calories: 348; Total Fat: 10g; Saturated Fat: 3g; Cholesterol: 70mg; Sodium: 753mg; Total Carbohydrates: 35g; Fiber: 12g; Protein: 33g

Basic Chili

SERVES 4 TO 6 • PREP TIME: 10 MINUTES
COOK TIME: 8 HOURS

1 pound lean ground beef

1 medium yellow onion, finely diced

3 (10-ounce) cans diced tomatoes with green chiles

2 (15-ounce) cans kidney beans, rinsed and drained

¼ cup tomato paste

2 teaspoons ground cumin

1½ teaspoons chili powder

Salt

Freshly ground black pepper

Optional toppings: shredded sharp Cheddar cheese, sour cream, chopped scallions, crumbled corn chips

This chili is a very simple recipe—so simple I think even my 11-year-old daughter could make it. When we serve chili, we like to top it with shredded sharp Cheddar cheese and some crumbled corn chips, and sometimes I make a sour cream corn bread to go with it.

1 Put the ground beef in the slow cooker. Use a wooden spoon to break up the meat into chunks.

2 Add the onion, tomatoes with their juice, beans, tomato paste, cumin, and chili powder. Season with salt and pepper and stir to combine.

3 Cover and cook on low for 8 hours.

4 Stir and break up any large chunks of meat. Season with additional salt and pepper, if desired. Ladle into bowls and serve with your favorite toppings.

SUPER EASY To make this recipe even faster, use frozen chopped onions. You can find them next to the other frozen vegetables at your grocery store. These come in handy, especially if you get very teary-eyed while chopping onions.

PER SERVING Calories: 504; Total Fat: 12g; Saturated Fat: 5g; Cholesterol: 75mg; Sodium: 1,444mg; Total Carbohydrates: 58g; Fiber: 20g; Protein: 42g

Vegetarian Chili

SERVES 6 • PREP TIME: 15 MINUTES
COOK TIME: 8 HOURS

**BIG 8 ALLERGEN FREE
SET AND FORGET**

2 (15-ounce) cans kidney or pinto
beans, rinsed and drained

1 (14.5-ounce) can diced tomatoes
with green peppers and onions

1 (16-ounce) jar chunky salsa

1 sweet potato, peeled
and cut into cubes

½ cup water

2 tablespoons tomato paste

1 teaspoon garlic powder

1 teaspoon ground cumin

1 teaspoon chili powder

Salt

Freshly ground black pepper

This vegetarian chili is meatless, but definitely not flavorless. For further enhancement, you can top your chili with some of these flavorful toppings: chopped fresh cilantro, diced red onions or scallions, guacamole, shredded cheese, sour cream, or crushed corn chips.

1 Combine all the ingredients in the slow cooker and stir to combine.

2 Cover and cook on low for 8 hours.

3 Season with additional salt and pepper, if needed. Ladle into bowls and serve.

SUPER EASY Sometimes my grocery store has packages of sweet potatoes or butternut squash that is already peeled and cut up. Using this convenience product helps me get this recipe into the slow cooker even faster.

PER SERVING Calories: 324; Total Fat: 2g; Saturated Fat: 0g; Cholesterol: 0mg; Sodium: 1,717mg; Total Carbohydrates: 64g; Fiber: 20g; Protein: 18g

Spicy Pork Chili

SERVES 6 • PREP TIME: 10 MINUTES
COOK TIME: 8 HOURS

**BIG 8 ALLERGEN FREE
SET AND FORGET**

**3 (15-ounce) cans black-eyed peas,
rinsed and drained, divided**

2 cups chicken broth, divided

2 medium yellow onions, finely diced

1 tablespoon chili powder

2 teaspoons garlic powder

1 teaspoon ground cumin

2 tablespoons tomato paste

2 tablespoons brown sugar

**1 tablespoon minced canned
chipotle chiles in adobo sauce**

**1½ pounds boneless country-style
pork ribs, trimmed of excess fat,
and cut into bite-size pieces**

Salt

Freshly ground black pepper

They say that black-eyed peas eaten on New Year's Day will bring you good luck. I'm not sure I believe in superstitions, but this spicy pork chili would be a perfect dish to eat on any January day. I use country-style pork ribs for this recipe because they are lean (and that's what is on our mind in January, right?!) and because they become tender in the slow cooker over many hours.

1 In a blender, combine 1 can of the black-eyed peas and 1 cup of the broth and process until smooth and creamy. Transfer to the slow cooker.

2 Stir in the remaining black-eyed peas and broth. Add the onions, chili powder, garlic powder, cumin, tomato paste, brown sugar, chipotle chiles, and pork.

3 Cover and cook on low for 8 hours.

4 Stir and season with salt and pepper. Ladle into bowls and serve.

INGREDIENT TIP You'll use only a partial can of the chipotle chiles for this recipe. Save the rest for another day by freezing it. Line a rimmed baking sheet with parchment paper or aluminum foil. Place each leftover chile on the paper or foil. Add a generous spoonful of adobo sauce to cover each pepper. Put the baking sheet in the freezer for 30 minutes to 1 hour, until the peppers and sauce are frozen. Gently remove each frozen chipotle pepper and sauce from the baking sheet, and wrap it in torn pieces of the parchment or foil. Store the wrapped peppers in a resealable plastic freezer bag until ready to use, for up to 3 months.

PER SERVING Calories: 358; Total Fat: 15g; Saturated Fat: 3g; Cholesterol: 85mg; Sodium: 403mg; Total Carbohydrates: 25g; Fiber: 6g; Protein: 31g

Old-Fashioned Chicken Stew

SERVES 6 • PREP TIME: 10 MINUTES
COOK TIME: 8 HOURS

**BIG 8 ALLERGEN FREE
SET AND FORGET**

4 cups chicken broth

2 cups frozen mirepoix

3 tablespoons tomato paste

1 teaspoon garlic powder

½ teaspoon dried thyme

¾ teaspoon salt, plus
more for seasoning

2 bay leaves

**4 russet potatoes, peeled
(about 1½ pounds)**

**2 pounds boneless, skinless chicken
thighs, trimmed of excess fat**

1 cup frozen peas

Freshly ground black pepper

This chicken stew is an old-fashioned favorite. After the stew is cooked, some of the potatoes are mashed to thicken the soup and give it more body without using flour or cornstarch. I like to serve this stew with homemade biscuits.

1 Combine the broth, mirepoix, tomato paste, garlic powder, thyme, salt, and bay leaves in the slow cooker. Stir to combine. Nestle the potatoes and the chicken in the slow cooker.

2 Cover and cook on low for 8 hours.

3 Transfer the chicken to a cutting board. Shred the chicken with two forks. Return the chicken to the slow cooker.

4 Transfer the potatoes to the cutting board. Use a fork to mash two of the potatoes. Cut the remaining two potatoes into cubes. Return the mashed and cubed potatoes to the slow cooker. Stir to combine. Add the frozen peas and let it sit until heated through, about 5 minutes.

5 Discard the bay leaves. Season the chili with additional salt and pepper, if needed, and serve.

SIMPLE SWAP If you can't find frozen mirepoix in your local grocery store, you can make your own. Traditional mirepoix consists of two parts onions, one part carrots, and one part celery. Dice the veggies and combine them, then freeze on a rimmed baking sheet lined with parchment paper or aluminum foil. Let them freeze for a couple of hours, then transfer the frozen veggie mixture to a resealable plastic freezer bag. Now whenever you need to start a soup with this trio of veggies, it will be ready for you.

PER SERVING Calories: 359; Total Fat: 9g; Saturated Fat: 2g; Cholesterol: 107mg; Sodium: 981mg; Total Carbohydrates: 32g; Fiber: 7g; Protein: 38g

Beef Stroganoff

SERVES 4 TO 6 • PREP TIME: 15 MINUTES
COOK TIME: 8 HOURS

SET AND FORGET

2 medium yellow onions, cut into very thin half moons

1 teaspoon sugar

1 pound white button mushrooms, sliced

2 pounds beef chuck roast, cut into bite-size pieces

1 teaspoon garlic powder

1 teaspoon onion powder

½ teaspoon salt

1 cup beef broth

1½ cups sour cream

1 tablespoon all-purpose flour

Cooked egg noodles, for serving

This simple version of beef stroganoff is one of my favorite comfort foods. There are many variations you can make of this dish. My mom often used ground beef recipe instead of beef chuck roast. You can also make this dish into a chicken stroganoff by using bite-size pieces of boneless, skinless chicken thighs.

1 Put the onions in the slow cooker. Sprinkle with the sugar and stir.

2 Add the sliced mushrooms and beef. Sprinkle in the garlic powder, onion powder, and salt. Pour the beef broth over the top.

3 Cover and cook on low for 8 hours.

4 In a small bowl, whisk together the sour cream and flour. Stir the sour cream mixture into the stew. Turn the slow cooker to high and cook with the lid off for about 10 minutes to thicken the sauce.

5 Serve the beef stroganoff over the egg noodles.

SIMPLE SWAP I used white button mushrooms for this stroganoff, but you can use cremini (baby bella) mushrooms, if you prefer. For this dish, you can also use frozen mushrooms or canned mushrooms if you don't have fresh on hand.

ALLERGY TIP If you're allergic to dairy, you can substitute vegan sour cream for the dairy sour cream.

PER SERVING Calories: 596; Total Fat: 35g; Saturated Fat: 16g; Cholesterol: 178mg; Sodium: 686mg; Total Carbohydrates: 16g; Fiber: 3g; Protein: 55g

Hearty Pork Stew

SERVES 6 • PREP TIME: 15 MINUTES
COOK TIME: 8½ HOURS

SET AND FORGET

1½ pounds boneless pork loin roast, cut into 1-inch pieces

2 cups frozen mirepoix

1½ cups cubed peeled russet potatoes or sweet potatoes

4 cups chicken broth

1 teaspoon dried sage

¾ teaspoon dried thyme

½ teaspoon salt

½ teaspoon freshly ground black pepper

3 tablespoons all-purpose flour

3 tablespoons unsalted butter, melted

My favorite way to round out this hearty stew is to serve warm homemade biscuits. If you don't have the time (or energy) to make biscuits from scratch, feel free to use refrigerator biscuits instead.

1 Combine the pork, mirepoix, potatoes, broth, sage, thyme, salt, and pepper in the slow cooker.

2 Cover and cook on low for 8 hours.

3 In a small bowl, whisk together the flour and butter. Stir the mixture into the juices in the slow cooker. Cover and turn to high. Let the stew thicken for about 30 minutes. Ladle into bowls and serve.

ALLERGY TIP If you're allergic to wheat, substitute gluten-free flour for the flour. If you're allergic to dairy, substitute olive oil for the butter.

PER SERVING Calories: 295; Total Fat: 15g; Saturated Fat: 7g; Cholesterol: 70mg; Sodium: 1,148mg; Total Carbohydrates: 14g; Fiber: 1g; Protein: 26g

5

MEATLESS MEALS

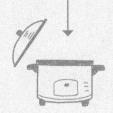

Mexican Beans and Rice

SERVES 4 • PREP TIME: 5 MINUTES
COOK TIME: 3 HOURS

BIG 8 ALLERGEN FREE

1 (15-ounce) can black beans, rinsed and drained

¾ cup long-grain brown rice

1½ cups water

¾ cup salsa or picante sauce, plus more if desired

1 bay leaf

1 teaspoon ground cumin

½ teaspoon garlic powder

½ teaspoon salt

1 to 2 tablespoons fresh lime juice

Sour cream, for topping (optional)

This dish can be a meal in itself or a side dish for a large Mexican meal. The recipe can easily be doubled. Because this recipe takes only 3 hours to prepare, I often put all the ingredients into the slow cooker when my kids are arriving home from school at about 3 p.m. and start the cook time then. And if I'm not home to turn the slow cooker on, I just have my kids turn it to low.

1 Combine the beans, rice, water, salsa, bay leaf, cumin, garlic powder, and salt in the slow cooker.

2 Cover and cook on low for 3 hours.

3 Discard the bay leaf. Add the lime juice and additional salsa, if desired.

4 Serve with a dollop of sour cream (if using).

SIMPLE SWAP If you don't have a can of black beans on hand, you can substitute pinto beans for the black beans.

PER SERVING Calories: 262; Total Fat: 2g; Saturated Fat: 0g; Cholesterol: 0mg; Sodium: 587mg; Total Carbohydrates: 52g; Fiber: 10g; Protein: 11g

Spaghetti Squash with Feta

SERVES 2 • PREP TIME: 5 MINUTES
COOK TIME: 6 HOURS

1 small (1- to 2-pound) spaghetti squash

1 cup water

¼ cup heavy cream

3 garlic cloves, minced

3 tablespoons unsalted butter

½ cup feta cheese

Salt

Freshly ground black pepper

2 tablespoons chopped fresh parsley, for garnish

Spaghetti squash is a wonderful low-calorie option for those of us who love pasta but don't want to eat all those carb calories. After it is cooked, you can shred the flesh and it resembles spaghetti. It's very mild tasting, so it takes on whatever flavor of sauce you decide to serve with it. I love cooking spaghetti squash in the slow cooker because it's a no-fuss method that requires literally 2 minutes of up-front work.

1 Using a sharp knife, make 6 to 8 slits all over the spaghetti squash. Place the squash in the slow cooker. Add the water.

2 Cover and cook on low for 6 hours.

3 Transfer the squash to a cutting board and allow it to cool slightly. Once you can handle it, slice the squash lengthwise and scoop out the seeds. Using a fork, scrape the flesh to create long strands resembling spaghetti.

4 Return the squash strands to the slow cooker and turn to low. Add the cream, garlic, and butter and stir gently to combine. Add the feta. Season with salt and pepper. Garnish with chopped parsley and serve.

INGREDIENT TIP If you have extra parsley and you don't think you'll use it up before it goes bad, you can freeze it! Parsley can be frozen by the bunch in freezer bags, chopped up, and made into ice cubes, or processed as pesto before freezing.

ALLERGY TIP If you're allergic to dairy, you can serve the spaghetti squash with a traditional spaghetti sauce instead of cream and feta cheese.

PER SERVING Calories: 453; Total Fat: 34g; Saturated Fat: 21g; Cholesterol: 100mg; Sodium: 705mg; Total Carbohydrates: 35g; Fiber: 0g; Protein: 9g

Zucchini Noodles with Marinara Sauce

SERVES 6 • PREP TIME: 15 MINUTES
COOK TIME: 8 HOURS

BIG 8 ALLERGEN FREE
SET AND FORGET

2 (28-ounce) cans crushed tomatoes

1 (14.5-ounce) can diced tomatoes with green peppers and onion

1 (6-ounce) can tomato paste

1 bay leaf

2 teaspoons dried basil

1 teaspoon garlic powder

½ teaspoon dried oregano

1 teaspoon brown sugar

2 tablespoons olive oil

Salt

Freshly ground black pepper

4 medium zucchini, trimmed

I like to serve this marinara sauce with "zoodles" for a change of pace, although it's also delicious with whole-wheat angel hair pasta. And to make it extra special, sometimes I make garlic bread to serve alongside.

1 Combine the crushed tomatoes, diced tomatoes with their juice, tomato paste, bay leaf, basil, garlic powder, oregano, and brown sugar in the slow cooker. Stir to combine.

2 Cover and cook on low for 8 hours.

3 Discard the bay leaf. Stir in the olive oil. Season with salt and pepper.

4 Using a spiralizer, make zucchini noodles. (If you don't have a spiralizer, use a potato peeler.) Place the zucchini noodles in a microwave-safe dish and microwave on high for 3 minutes. Pile the zucchini on individual serving plates and top with marinara sauce.

SIMPLE SWAP To make this marinara sauce brighter, use fresh basil and oregano. Just triple the amount of dried herbs called for in the recipe. Don't add them to the slow cooker until you stir in the olive oil or their flavor will just get washed out.

PER SERVING Calories: 156; Total Fat: 5g; Saturated Fat: 1g; Cholesterol: 0mg; Sodium: 422mg; Total Carbohydrates: 24g; Fiber: 8g; Protein: 7g

Coconut Curry with Vegetables

SERVES 4 • PREP TIME: 5 MINUTES
COOK TIME: 4 HOURS

BIG 8 ALLERGEN FREE

1 (13.5-ounce) can
coconut milk, stirred

2 tablespoons red curry paste

2 tablespoons instant tapioca

1 (1-pound) package frozen
stir-fry vegetables

1 (15-ounce) can chickpeas,
rinsed and drained

Salt

Freshly ground black pepper

I am a huge fan of curry, and this recipe is easy to make. The coconut milk contributes a delicious, smooth richness. We like to serve this curry over quinoa or brown rice.

1 Combine the coconut milk, curry paste, and tapioca in the slow cooker. Stir until the curry paste is thoroughly blended into the milk. Stir in the vegetables and chickpeas.

2 Cover and cook on low for 4 hours.

3 Season with salt and pepper and serve.

INGREDIENT TIP Look for canned coconut milk that doesn't have added sugar or thickeners. Coconut milk tends to separate in the can, so before opening the can, submerge it in hot water for 15 minutes. Then open the can and stir before using.

PER SERVING Calories: 483; Total Fat: 28g; Saturated Fat: 23g; Cholesterol: 0mg; Sodium: 780mg; Total Carbohydrates: 50g; Fiber: 11g; Protein: 10g

Mexican Quinoa Bowl

SERVES 4 • PREP TIME: 10 MINUTES
COOK TIME: 3 HOURS

BIG 8 ALLERGEN FREE

1 cup quinoa, rinsed and drained

1½ cups water

**1 (10-ounce) can diced
tomatoes with green chiles**

**1 (15-ounce) can black beans,
rinsed and drained**

2 tablespoons fresh lime juice

1 teaspoon garlic powder

½ teaspoon salt

Freshly ground black pepper

1 avocado, peeled, pitted, and sliced

Quinoa is one of my favorite healthy foods. It is an ancient grain that originated in the mountains of South America. It is just as satisfying as a bowl of rice but provides more protein and nutrients. It is also gluten-free and is one of the few plant foods that contains all nine essential amino acids.

1 Combine the quinoa, water, diced tomatoes with their juices, black beans, lime juice, garlic powder, and salt in the slow cooker.

2 Cover and cook on low for 3 hours. Remove the lid and fluff the ingredients with a fork. Season with additional salt and pepper, if needed.

3 Scoop the quinoa and vegetables into serving bowls. Top each portion with avocado slices and serve.

INGREDIENT TIP How do you know when an avocado is ready to eat? Place the avocado in the palm of your hand and gently squeeze without applying your fingertips, because that can cause bruising. If the avocado yields to firm, gentle pressure, you know it's ripe and ready to eat.

INGREDIENT TIP Always rinse quinoa until the water runs clear before cooking. The seeds have a bitter coating that needs to be washed off.

PER SERVING Calories: 395; Total Fat: 13g; Saturated Fat: 3g; Cholesterol: 0mg; Sodium: 505mg; Total Carbohydrates: 57g; Fiber: 15g; Protein: 61g

Baked Potatoes with Avocado Pico de Gallo

SERVES 6 • PREP TIME: 5 MINUTES
COOK TIME: 8 HOURS

**BIG 8 ALLERGEN FREE
SET AND FORGET**

6 russet potatoes

2 tablespoons olive oil

⅓ cup finely chopped red onion

4 Roma tomatoes, finely chopped

⅓ cup chopped fresh cilantro

1 ripe avocado, peeled, pitted, and finely chopped

Salt

Freshly ground black pepper

Making "baked" potatoes in the slow cooker is one of my favorite ways to use the magical appliance. Wrap each in aluminum foil to keep them super moist. You can pile in as many potatoes as you can fit. Baked potatoes topped with pico de gallo (or salsa fresca) are heavenly.

1 Scrub the potatoes thoroughly and dry with paper towels. Pierce each with a fork in several places. Rub them with olive oil. Wrap each potato tightly in aluminum foil. Put the potatoes in the slow cooker.

2 Cover and cook on low for 8 hours, or until the potatoes are tender when pierced with a fork. Remove the wrapped potatoes from the slow cooker, cover with a towel to keep warm, and set aside.

3 To prepare the pico de gallo, in a medium bowl, gently stir together the onion, tomatoes, cilantro, and avocado. Season with salt and pepper.

4 Unwrap each potato and halve lengthwise. Fluff the potato flesh with a fork. Top each potato with a generous portion of pico de gallo and serve.

TASTY TIP A favorite trick of mine for adding flavor to this dish is to scoop ¼ cup of full-fat cottage cheese on top of my potato and then plop the pico de gallo on top of that. It adds protein and fat, which makes for a satisfying meal.

PER SERVING Calories: 410; Total Fat: 12g; Saturated Fat: 2g; Cholesterol: 0mg; Sodium: 50mg; Total Carbohydrates: 72g; Fiber: 8g; Protein: 9g

Southwestern Stuffed Bell Peppers

SERVES 6 • PREP TIME: 15 MINUTES
COOK TIME: 6 HOURS

6 bell peppers (any color)

2 (15-ounce) cans pinto beans, rinsed and drained

1 cup quinoa, rinsed and drained

1½ cups red or green enchilada sauce

1 teaspoon ground cumin

1 teaspoon chili powder

1 teaspoon onion powder

¾ teaspoon salt

½ teaspoon garlic powder

1½ cups shredded Mexican cheese, divided

½ cup water

Stuffed bell peppers are one of those meals that don't really need anything to go with them. They contain protein, starch, and fat, and the peppers provide many vitamins and minerals. And they are fun to make. The bell peppers are hollowed out, the stuffing is packed inside, and they are slowly cooked to a unique, delicious flavor.

1 Cut off the top of each bell pepper. Scrape out the seeds and ribs.

2 Pour one can of pinto beans into a large bowl. Use a fork to smash the beans so they resemble refried beans. Add the other can of beans to the bowl. Add the quinoa, enchilada sauce, cumin, chili powder, onion powder, salt, garlic powder, and 1 cup of cheese. Stir the mixture together until combined.

3 Pour the water into the slow cooker. Fill each pepper with the bean mixture and place the peppers standing up in the water. Let them lean against each other if needed.

4 Cover and cook on low for 6 hours. Remove the lid and sprinkle the remaining ½ cup of cheese on top of the peppers. Cover until the cheese is melted. Serve hot.

SIMPLE SWAP   You can substitute black beans for the pinto beans or use one can of each, or try one can of refried beans and one can of pinto beans.

INGREDIENT TIP   Some optional toppings you may like with your stuffed peppers are sour cream, guacamole, and pico de gallo.

ALLERGY TIP   If you're allergic to cheese, you can use a vegan cheese instead or just leave out the cheese entirely.

PER SERVING Calories: 453; Total Fat: 15g; Saturated Fat: 7g; Cholesterol: 30mg; Sodium: 1,258mg; Total Carbohydrates: 60g; Fiber: 14g; Protein: 22g

Farro Risotto

SERVES 4 • PREP TIME: 15 MINUTES
COOK TIME: 4 HOURS

Nonstick cooking spray

2¼ cups vegetable broth

1 cup whole farro

1 medium yellow onion, finely diced

1 tablespoon unsalted butter

1 teaspoon garlic powder

3 carrots, peeled and grated

½ teaspoon salt, plus
more for seasoning

4 ounces goat cheese, crumbled

¼ cup boiling water, if needed

Freshly ground black pepper

Traditional risotto usually requires the cook's attention from start to finish. By using the slow cooker, you get a hands-off version that requires very little attention once the ingredients are added to it. This risotto replaces the traditional Arborio rice with farro, an ancient grain that is packed with nutrients, is pleasingly chewy, and has a delicious nutty flavor.

1 Lightly spray the inside of the slow cooker with nonstick cooking spray. Pour in the vegetable broth.

2 In a microwave-safe bowl, combine the farro, onion, butter, and garlic powder. Microwave on high for 5 minutes, stirring halfway through. Add the mixture to the slow cooker. In the slow cooker, stir in the carrots and salt.

3 Cover and cook on low for 4 hours.

4 If needed, stir in up to ¼ cup of boiling water to loosen the mixture. Crumble the goat cheese over the risotto. Season with additional salt and pepper, if desired, and serve.

INGREDIENT TIP This recipe uses whole, unprocessed farro. Do not substitute processed (pearl, quick-cooking, or presteamed) farro for the whole farro, or the recipe cook time won't be correct. You may need to carefully read the information on the package to establish whether the farro has been presteamed. Sometimes I can find whole farro in the bulk section of my grocery store.

SIMPLE SWAP If you don't care for goat cheese, you can substitute grated Parmesan cheese.

ALLERGY TIP If you're allergic to dairy, leave out the goat cheese or substitute a vegan cheese. If you're allergic to wheat, you can substitute brown rice for the farro.

PER SERVING Calories: 253; Total Fat: 14g; Saturated Fat: 9g; Cholesterol: 37mg; Sodium: 921mg; Total Carbohydrates: 17g; Fiber: 3g; Protein: 14g

Lentil and Bean Salad

SERVES 2 • PREP TIME: 10 MINUTES
COOK TIME: 4 HOURS

1 cup vegetable broth

1 (15-ounce) can pinto beans, rinsed and drained

⅔ cup brown lentils

3 tablespoons fresh lime juice, divided

1 teaspoon garlic powder

¼ teaspoon dried oregano

½ teaspoon salt, plus more for seasoning

6 ounces cherry tomatoes, halved

2 teaspoons olive oil

1 ounce queso fresco, crumbled

Freshly ground black pepper

I love making lentils in the slow cooker. They come to an almost creamy consistency but still maintain their shape. Serve this salad with some crusty sourdough bread. To add more vegetables to the meal, you can serve the lentils over salad greens. Queso fresco is a Mexican cheese that is creamy but not too rich, and the flavor is fresh and mild.

1 Combine the vegetable broth, beans, lentils, 1 tablespoon of lime juice, garlic powder, oregano, and salt in the slow cooker.

2 Cover and cook on low for 4 hours.

3 Stir in the remaining 2 tablespoons of lime juice, cherry tomatoes, olive oil, and queso fresco. Season with additional salt and pepper, if desired, and serve.

INGREDIENT TIP I like to freeze fresh lime juice for later use. When limes are on sale, I buy a big bag and juice them all at the same time into a mason jar. Then I freeze the lime juice. When I need a tablespoon or two for a recipe, I'll stick the glass jar (minus the metal lid) in the microwave for 30 seconds. This melts the lime juice just enough for me to pour off the small amount I need. I do the same with lemons!

ALLERGY TIP If you're allergic to dairy, you can replace the queso fresco with a vegan cheese.

PER SERVING Calories: 613; Total Fat: 12g; Saturated Fat: 4g; Cholesterol: 11mg; Sodium: 1,099mg; Total Carbohydrates: 100g; Fiber: 38g; Protein: 39g

Ratatouille

SERVES 4 • PREP TIME: 15 MINUTES
COOK TIME: 5 HOURS

BIG 8 ALLERGEN FREE

1 medium yellow onion, diced

2 tablespoons olive oil, divided

1 tablespoon tomato paste

2 teaspoons garlic powder

1 teaspoon dried basil

¼ teaspoon salt, plus
more for seasoning

**8 ounces eggplant, cut
into 1-inch dice**

8 ounces zucchini, cut into 1-inch dice

**1 large red, yellow, or orange
bell pepper, seeded and
cut into 1-inch pieces**

Freshly ground black pepper

Ratatouille is a French Provençal stewed vegetable dish. This simple slow cooker version can be a complete meal with some Parmesan cheese sprinkled on the top. It is also delicious spooned onto toasted garlic bread, or it can be tossed with freshly cooked pasta for an easy summer meal.

1 Combine the onion and 1 tablespoon of olive oil in a microwave-safe bowl. Cover and microwave on high for 5 minutes, stirring halfway through. Stir in the tomato paste, garlic powder, basil, salt, and the remaining 1 tablespoon of olive oil. Pour the mixture into the slow cooker. Add the eggplant, zucchini, and bell pepper and stir.

2 Cover and cook on low for 5 hours.

3 Season with additional salt and pepper, if desired, and serve.

INGREDIENT TIP I always think it's funny to see baseball bat–size zucchini. Many delicious items can be made from those big zucchini, but they are not suitable for ratatouille. For this recipe, select small to medium zucchini that are firm all over, especially on the flower end (the opposite end from the stem), and feel heavy for their size. The skin should be shiny and smooth, with a bright, even, green color and no blemishes.

PER SERVING Calories: 135; Total Fat: 8g; Saturated Fat: 1g; Cholesterol: 0mg; Sodium: 171mg; Total Carbohydrates: 17g; Fiber: 6g; Protein: 4g

Chapter

6

CHICKEN

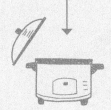

Whole Seasoned Chicken

SERVES 6 TO 8 • PREP TIME: 10 MINUTES
COOK TIME: 8 HOURS

SET AND FORGET

1 large onion, cut into thick slices

6 garlic cloves, lightly smashed

1 cup chicken broth

3 tablespoons unsalted butter, melted

1 teaspoon dried rosemary

1 teaspoon dried sage

½ teaspoon dried thyme

1 teaspoon salt

¼ teaspoon freshly ground black pepper

1 (5-pound) chicken

This chicken preparation reminds me of the rotisserie chicken you can get at the grocery store. It's tender, moist, and well seasoned. I usually serve this chicken with a side salad or some mashed potatoes. I love using the leftover chicken for chicken salad or any recipe that calls for cooked chicken.

1 Combine the onion, garlic, and chicken broth in the slow cooker.

2 In a small bowl, stir together the butter, rosemary, sage, thyme, salt, and pepper. Rub the spice mixture all over the chicken (make sure the chicken is dry before you do this). Place the chicken, breast-side down, on top of the onion.

3 Cover and cook on low for 8 hours, or until the thickest part of the chicken thigh reaches a temperature of 165°F.

4 Carefully remove the chicken and place it on a platter or a rimmed baking sheet. Loosely tent the chicken with aluminum foil and let it rest for 10 minutes. Discard the onion, garlic, and broth.

TASTY TIP   If you want to crisp up the skin on the chicken, turn on the broiler. Carefully place the cooked chicken on a rimmed baking sheet or in a roaster pan. Broil for several minutes, until the skin is crispy and brown, watching it carefully to make sure it doesn't burn.

ALLERGY TIP   If you are allergic to dairy, use olive oil instead of butter.

PER SERVING Calories: 716; Total Fat: 51g; Saturated Fat: 17g; Cholesterol: 269mg; Sodium: 771mg; Total Carbohydrates: 4g; Fiber: 1g; Protein: 57g

Cheesy Barbecued Chicken Spaghetti

SERVES 4 TO 6 • PREP TIME: 5 MINUTES
COOK TIME: 8 HOURS

SET AND FORGET

2 pounds bone-in, skinless chicken thighs, trimmed of excess fat

2 cups tomato sauce

½ cup barbecue sauce

8 ounces angel hair pasta

2 cups shredded sharp Cheddar cheese

This cheesy angel hair pasta is a kids' favorite. If you want to use a different type of pasta, you can. Just cook the pasta on the stove according to the package directions, and add it to the slow cooker after the chicken has cooked.

1 Put the chicken in the slow cooker.

2 In a large bowl, mix the tomato sauce and barbecue sauce. Pour the sauce over the chicken.

3 Cover and cook on low for 8 hours.

4 Carefully transfer the chicken to a cutting board.

5 Break the angel hair pasta into 1-inch pieces. Add them to the slow cooker. Stir the sauce over the noodles. Cover and turn the slow cooker to high for 10 minutes.

6 Remove the bones and cartilage from the chicken. Shred the chicken with two forks or cut it into small pieces.

7 Once the pasta is cooked through (about 10 minutes), return the shredded chicken to the slow cooker and stir in the cheese. Scoop onto serving plates and serve.

SIMPLE SWAP Instead of Cheddar cheese, you can use a mix of other types of cheeses, like Parmesan and mozzarella.

ALLERGY TIP If you are sensitive to dairy, replace the Cheddar with a vegan cheese.

PER SERVING Calories: 699; Total Fat: 27g; Saturated Fat: 14g; Cholesterol: 202mg; Sodium: 1,517mg; Total Carbohydrates: 57g; Fiber: 6g; Protein: 59g

Chicken Gyros

SERVES 6 • PREP TIME: 10 MINUTES
COOK TIME: 8 HOURS

SET AND FORGET

2 pounds boneless, skinless chicken thighs, trimmed of excess fat

1 large onion, halved and thinly sliced

¼ cup olive oil

2 tablespoons fresh lemon juice

2 teaspoons garlic powder

1 teaspoon dried oregano

½ teaspoon salt, plus more for seasoning

¼ teaspoon freshly ground black pepper, plus more for seasoning

6 pita breads, warmed

Tzatziki sauce, for serving

Optional toppings: chopped lettuce, tomatoes, red bell peppers, and cucumbers

I often serve chicken gyros as an all-in-one meal. I stuff as much lettuce and tomato into each pita to make it as healthy as possible. Sometimes I slice up red bell peppers and cucumbers, and add them to the pita as well. Of course, I always top everything with a large dollop of tzatziki sauce.

1 Put the chicken and onion in the slow cooker.

2 In a small bowl, whisk together the olive oil, lemon juice, garlic powder, oregano, salt, and pepper. Pour the mixture over the chicken and onion and toss to coat.

3 Cover and cook on low for 8 hours, or until the chicken is tender.

4 Transfer the chicken to a cutting board. Shred the chicken with two forks, then return it to the slow cooker. Stir.

5 Season with additional salt and pepper, if needed. Serve the chicken and onions with pita breads, and pass the tzatziki sauce and chopped vegetables, if desired.

INGREDIENT TIP You can easily make your own tzatziki sauce. Just stir together 1 cup plain Greek yogurt, 1 seeded and diced cucumber, 1 tablespoon fresh lemon juice, 1 minced garlic clove, 1 tablespoon dried dill, and plenty of salt and pepper. Store the leftover sauce in an airtight container in the refrigerator for up to 3 days.

ALLERGY TIP If you're allergic to dairy, forgo the tzatziki sauce. If you're allergic to wheat, serve the gyro chicken wrapped in a large lettuce leaf.

PER SERVING Calories: 338; Total Fat: 15g; Saturated Fat: 3g; Cholesterol: 127mg; Sodium: 480mg; Total Carbohydrates: 19g; Fiber: 1g; Protein: 32g

Coconut Chicken Drumsticks

SERVES 5 • PREP TIME: 10 MINUTES
COOK TIME: 6 HOURS

BIG 8 ALLERGEN FREE

1 (13.5-ounce) can
coconut milk, stirred

2 tablespoons Sriracha sauce

1 tablespoon Thai garlic chili paste

1 tablespoon tamari or low-
sodium soy sauce

1 teaspoon dried basil

3 to 4 pounds chicken drumsticks

Steamed rice, for serving (optional)

Chopped fresh cilantro,
for garnish (optional)

You can make this recipe into a slow cooker freezer meal! Just toss all the ingredients into a gallon-size, resealable, plastic freezer bag, seal, and freeze. When you're ready to cook, drop everything from the bag into the slow cooker and cook on low for 8 hours if still frozen or for 6 hours if thawed. The chicken will be very tender.

1 Combine the coconut milk, Sriracha sauce, Thai garlic chili paste, and tamari in the slow cooker. Stir to combine.

2 Using a double layer of paper towels, pull the skin off the chicken drumsticks. Add the now skinless chicken drumsticks to the slow cooker, nestling them into the sauce.

3 Cover and cook on low for 6 hours.

4 If desired, serve the chicken and sauce over rice and garnish with cilantro.

SIMPLE SWAP You can use bone-in chicken thighs in the place of the drumsticks for this dish, if you wish. Just remove the skin on the chicken thighs first and trim any excess fat.

PER SERVING Calories: 638; Total Fat: 38g; Saturated Fat: 21g; Cholesterol: 257mg; Sodium: 593mg; Total Carbohydrates: 6g; Fiber: 2g; Protein: 72g

Garlic-Lime Chicken

SERVES 4 • PREP TIME: 5 MINUTES
COOK TIME: 6 HOURS

BIG 8 ALLERGEN FREE

2 pounds boneless, skinless chicken thighs, trimmed of excess fat

½ cup tamari or low-sodium soy sauce

¼ cup fresh lime juice

1 tablespoon Worcestershire sauce

2 garlic cloves, minced

1 tablespoon brown sugar

½ teaspoon freshly ground black pepper

2 tablespoons cornstarch

2 tablespoons water

We love to serve this Asian-inspired chicken with brown rice and a green salad. If you have bone-in chicken thighs or drumsticks, those work just as well as the boneless thighs. Just remove the skin before placing them in the slow cooker.

1 Put the chicken thighs in the slow cooker.

2 In a medium bowl, whisk together the tamari, lime juice, Worcestershire sauce, garlic, brown sugar, and pepper. Pour the mixture over the chicken.

3 Cover and cook on low for 6 hours, or until the chicken is tender.

4 Turn the slow cooker to high. In a small bowl, whisk together the cornstarch and water. Stir the cornstarch slurry into the liquid in the slow cooker. Let the sauce thicken for 10 minutes.

5 Serve the chicken with the sauce.

INGREDIENT TIP I use a garlic press to mince my garlic, but if you don't have one you can use a fork to mince garlic. Just peel the garlic clove and then press it with the tines of the fork. Scrape off the fork and press it through the clove again in the other direction. Repeat as many times as necessary until the garlic clove is as minced as you'd like, and then pick out the hard stem if necessary.

PER SERVING Calories: 315; Total Fat: 9g; Saturated Fat: 2g; Cholesterol: 190mg; Sodium: 2,254mg; Total Carbohydrates: 10g; Fiber: 1g; Protein: 48g

Chicken and Broccoli

SERVES 6 • PREP TIME: 10 MINUTES
COOK TIME: 6 HOURS

BIG 8 ALLERGY FREE

1 cup chicken broth

½ cup oyster sauce

¼ cup tamari or low-sodium soy sauce

¼ cup (packed) brown sugar

1 teaspoon toasted sesame oil

1 teaspoon garlic powder

2 pounds boneless, skinless chicken thighs, trimmed of excess fat and cut into bite-size pieces

2 tablespoons cornstarch

2 tablespoons water

1 (16-ounce) package frozen broccoli florets

I'm a big fan of ordering beef and broccoli whenever I go out to a Chinese restaurant. This is a version of that dish, made with chicken instead. Tender pieces of chicken and a super savory sauce with semi-cooked broccoli all go together nicely over steamed white rice.

1 Combine the chicken broth, oyster sauce, tamari, brown sugar, sesame oil, and garlic powder in the slow cooker. Whisk until smooth. Add the chicken pieces and stir to coat with the sauce.

2 Cover and cook on low for 6 hours, or until the chicken is tender.

3 Remove the lid and turn the cooker to high. Make a cornstarch slurry by whisking the cornstarch and water together in a small bowl. Add the slurry to the liquid in the slow cooker and whisk until dissolved.

4 Pour the broccoli into a colander. Run hot water over the broccoli until it's warmed through. Shake off the excess water and then stir the broccoli into the slow cooker. Cover and cook on high for 10 minutes, or until the broccoli is cooked through and the sauce is thickened by the cornstarch. Serve.

SIMPLE SWAP If you would rather use fresh broccoli, just cut up 1 pound of broccoli into florets. Put the broccoli in a microwave-safe bowl and cover it with water. Place the bowl in the microwave oven, cover, and cook on high for 5 minutes. Drain off all the water and add the broccoli to the slow cooker.

PER SERVING Calories: 251; Total Fat: 7g; Saturated Fat: 2g; Cholesterol: 127mg; Sodium: 1,199mg; Total Carbohydrates: 13g; Fiber: 2g; Protein: 33g

Honey-Garlic Chicken

SERVES 4 TO 6 • PREP TIME: 10 MINUTES
COOK TIME: 6 HOURS

2 pounds boneless or bone-in, skinless chicken thighs, trimmed of excess fat

¼ cup all-purpose flour

⅓ cup honey

⅓ cup tamari or low-sodium soy sauce

⅓ cup fresh lemon juice

1 tablespoon instant tapioca

2 teaspoons garlic powder

When I was growing up, my mom used to make a version of this dish in the oven. We used to call it Kaye's chicken because the original recipe came from my mom's friend Kaye. I've changed a few things and turned it into a slow cooker recipe. I love serving this robust saucy chicken over some rice with roasted or steamed broccoli on the side

1 Dredge the chicken thighs in the flour and put them in the slow cooker.

2 In a small bowl, whisk together the honey, tamari, lemon juice, tapioca, and garlic powder. Pour the sauce over the chicken.

3 Cover and cook on low for 6 hours, or until the chicken is tender. Serve the chicken with the sauce.

INGREDIENT TIP Before I measure out honey, I spray the measuring cup with nonstick cooking spray. Then when I empty the measuring cup full of honey, it slides right out instead of sticking to the sides of the measuring cup.

ALLERGY TIP If you're allergic to wheat, use a gluten-free flour to coat the chicken or forgo the flour altogether. Without flour, the sauce will be thinner, but you can thicken it with cornstarch at the end of the cooking time.

PER SERVING Calories: 413; Total Fat: 9g; Saturated Fat: 2g; Cholesterol: 190mg; Sodium: 1,546mg; Total Carbohydrates: 36g; Fiber: 1g; Protein: 48g

Kalua Chicken

SERVES 6 • PREP TIME: 5 MINUTES
COOK TIME: 6 HOURS

4 slices uncooked bacon

2 pounds boneless, skinless chicken thighs, trimmed of excess fat

1 teaspoon salt, plus
more for seasoning

1 teaspoon liquid smoke

Freshly ground black pepper

Slider buns or rolls, for serving

Kalua pork is a popular dish in Hawaiian culture, but I make a version that uses chicken instead, something that I always have in my freezer ready to be thawed. These little sandwiches are a perfect slow cooker summer meal. Serve with a side of corn on the cob and some coleslaw.

1 Line the bottom of the slow cooker with the bacon slices. Place the chicken thighs on top of the bacon. Sprinkle the salt and liquid smoke over the chicken.

2 Cover and cook on low for 6 hours, or until the chicken is very tender.

3 Transfer the chicken to a cutting board. Discard the bacon. Shred the chicken and place on a platter.

4 Season the chicken with additional salt and pepper, if needed. Serve the chicken with slider buns or rolls.

ALLERGY TIP If you're allergic to wheat, serve the chicken with gluten-free rolls or bread.

PER SERVING Calories: 362; Total Fat: 13g; Saturated Fat: 4g; Cholesterol: 141mg; Sodium: 1,020mg; Total Carbohydrates: 21g; Fiber: 1g; Protein: 38g

Barbecued Cream Cheese Chicken

SERVES 6 • PREP TIME: 5 MINUTES
COOK TIME: 4 HOURS

2 pounds boneless, skinless chicken breasts, trimmed of excess fat

1 cup chicken broth

4 ounces cream cheese

¾ cup barbecue sauce

Salad greens, for serving

Tender chicken breasts cooked in the slow cooker and then mixed with cream cheese and barbecue sauce make for an easy, tasty dish. It is perfect for serving in sandwiches, rolled up in tortillas, or scattered atop pizza.

1 Combine the chicken and chicken broth in the slow cooker. Cover and cook on low for 4 hours.

2 Transfer the chicken to a cutting board. Shred the chicken with two forks. Drain all the liquid out of the slow cooker. Return the shredded chicken to the slow cooker. Add the cream cheese and barbecue sauce. Stir, letting the cream cheese melt and coat the chicken. Serve the chicken over salad greens.

INGREDIENT TIP If you soften the cream cheese before you add it to the slow cooker, it will melt faster. To quickly soften cream cheese, simply put the unwrapped cream cheese on a plate and microwave on high for 15 seconds. (Don't cook for much longer than 15 seconds or the cream cheese will explode all over the microwave!)

ALLERGY TIP If you're allergic to dairy, use a vegan cream cheese.

PER SERVING Calories: 293; Total Fat: 13g; Saturated Fat: 6g; Cholesterol: 147mg; Sodium: 666mg; Total Carbohydrates: 12g; Fiber: 0g; Protein: 32g

Cream Cheese Chicken Sandwiches

SERVES 6 • PREP TIME: 10 MINUTES
COOK TIME: 6 HOURS

2 pounds boneless, skinless chicken thighs, trimmed of excess fat

½ cup chili sauce

¼ cup apricot preserves

4 ounces cream cheese, cut into cubes

6 hamburger buns or rolls, toasted

These sandwiches are totally addictive. The combination of chili sauce and apricot preserves seems a little unusual, but I promise you're going to love it. We like to serve our sandwiches with a side of coleslaw or corn on the cob. Sometimes if I'm feeling really ambitious, I make my own buns to serve the meat on.

1 Put the chicken in the slow cooker. Pour the chili sauce and apricot preserves over the chicken.

2 Cover and cook on low for 6 hours, or until the chicken is tender.

3 Transfer the chicken to a cutting board. Shred the chicken with two forks and return it to the slow cooker. Stir in the cream cheese until it blends in with the sauce.

4 Serve the chicken and sauce on the toasted buns.

TASTY TIP If you want to really enhance these sandwiches, serve caramelized onions on top of the chicken. The onions are sweet and really bring the sandwiches to a whole new flavor level.

ALLERGY TIP If you're allergic to dairy, just leave out the cream cheese or use a vegan cream cheese.

PER SERVING Calories: 394; Total Fat: 15g; Saturated Fat: 6g; Cholesterol: 147mg; Sodium: 908mg; Total Carbohydrates: 31g; Fiber: 1g; Protein: 35g

Hawaiian Chicken

SERVES 6 • PREP TIME: 5 MINUTES
COOK TIME: 6 HOURS

BIG 8 ALLERGEN FREE

2 pounds boneless, skinless chicken thighs, trimmed of excess fat

1 red bell pepper, seeded and diced

1 (16-ounce) bottle barbecue sauce

1 (8-ounce) can crushed pineapple, drained of excess juice

1 teaspoon garlic powder

Salt

Freshly ground black pepper

Steamed rice, for serving

Hawaiian chicken is a perfect slow cooker summer supper. When the weather is too warm for you to stand over a hot stove but you don't want to sacrifice flavor, put this delicious dish on your menu. We serve it with rice, cilantro, and a dash of hot sauce.

1 Combine the chicken, bell pepper, barbecue sauce, crushed pineapple, and garlic powder in the slow cooker. Season liberally with salt and pepper and stir to combine.

2 Cover and cook on low for 6 hours, or until the chicken is tender. Season with salt and pepper. Serve the chicken and sauce over the rice.

TASTY TIP If you want a thicker, richer sauce, you can reduce it a bit on the stove top. First transfer the chicken to a warm platter. Then pour the sauce into a saucepan and cook over medium heat, stirring often, until the sauce is thickened.

PER SERVING Calories: 308; Total Fat: 6g; Saturated Fat: 1g; Cholesterol: 147mg; Sodium: 1,007mg; Total Carbohydrates: 33g; Fiber: 1g; Protein: 30g

Salsa Chicken

SERVES 4 • PREP TIME: 5 MINUTES
COOK TIME: 6 HOURS

2 pounds boneless, skinless chicken thighs, trimmed of excess fat

1 cup salsa

1 teaspoon chili powder

1 teaspoon garlic powder

1 teaspoon ground cumin

2 tablespoons fresh lime juice

Salt

Freshly ground black pepper

¼ cup guacamole

¼ cup sour cream

My family never gets tired of eating anything with salsa, sour cream, and guacamole. We pair this shredded salsa chicken with rice or serve it on warmed tortillas. If you want to get fancy, top it with chopped fresh cilantro and serve it with a lime wedge.

1 Put the chicken in the slow cooker. Add the salsa, chili powder, garlic powder, and cumin. Stir to coat the chicken.

2 Cover and cook on low for 6 hours, or until the chicken is tender.

3 Transfer the chicken to a cutting board. Shred the chicken with two forks. Return the chicken to the slow cooker and stir in the lime juice. Season with salt and pepper.

4 Serve the chicken topped with guacamole and sour cream.

TASTY TIP There are so many different kinds of salsa at the grocery store these days. Get creative and try something new—maybe salsa verde or even a salsa that has black beans and corn mixed in it. If you love a sweet salsa, try mango salsa.

ALLERGY TIP If you're allergic to dairy, simply omit the sour cream.

PER SERVING Calories: 359; Total Fat: 16g; Saturated Fat: 4g; Cholesterol: 196mg; Sodium: 730mg; Total Carbohydrates: 9g; Fiber: 2g; Protein: 40g

Chicken Tacos

SERVES 6 • PREP TIME: 5 MINUTES
COOK TIME: 6 HOURS

BIG 8 ALLERGEN FREE

2 pounds boneless, skinless chicken thighs, trimmed of excess fat

Salt

Freshly ground black pepper

1 (10-ounce) can diced tomatoes with green chiles

1 teaspoon ground cumin

1 teaspoon garlic powder

Corn taco shells or soft flour tortillas

Optional toppings: shredded cheese, sour cream, guacamole, fresh lime juice, chopped fresh cilantro, shredded lettuce, diced tomatoes

Taco Tuesday could become "Slow Cooker Taco Tuesday" from now on at your house. I love to serve this tender chicken wrapped in a warm, soft flour tortilla with some shredded cheese, diced tomatoes, a dollop of sour cream, and crunchy lettuce.

1 Put the chicken in the slow cooker. Season the chicken with salt and pepper. Add the tomatoes with their juice, cumin, and garlic powder. Stir to combine.

2 Cover and cook on low for 6 hours, or until the chicken is tender.

3 Transfer the chicken to a cutting board. Shred the chicken with two forks. Return the chicken to the slow cooker and stir. Season with additional salt and pepper, if needed.

4 Serve the chicken in taco shells or tortillas with your favorite toppings.

SIMPLE SWAP If you prefer, you can use premade taco seasoning mix in place of the cumin, garlic powder, salt, and pepper. Just add 3 tablespoons of taco seasoning to the slow cooker along with the chicken and tomatoes.

PER SERVING Calories: 308; Total Fat: 11g; Saturated Fat: 2g; Cholesterol: 127mg; Sodium: 509mg; Total Carbohydrates: 22g; Fiber: 3g; Protein: 32g

Tomatillo Chicken

SERVES 6 • PREP TIME: 15 MINUTES
COOK TIME: 6 HOURS

BIG 8 ALLERGEN FREE

2 pounds boneless, skinless chicken thighs, trimmed of excess fat

2½ teaspoons ground cumin, divided

2 teaspoons dried oregano

1½ teaspoons garlic powder

1¾ teaspoons salt, divided

½ teaspoon freshly ground black pepper

8 tomatillos, husked and halved

1 red onion, cut into wedges

1 poblano chile, cut into quarters and seeded

2 teaspoons fresh lime juice

This delicious dish features tender, moist shredded chicken with an almost creamy (but not too rich) tomatillo-based sauce. It is perfect for tacos, enchiladas, burritos, or salads—or just on its own.

1 Put the chicken in the slow cooker. Sprinkle with 2 teaspoons of cumin, the oregano, garlic powder, 1 teaspoon of salt, and the black pepper. Nestle the tomatillo halves, onion wedges, and poblano pieces around the chicken.

2 Cover and cook on low for 6 hours, or until the chicken is tender.

3 Transfer the chicken to a cutting board. Shred the chicken with two forks.

4 Carefully pour the mixture in the cooker through a fine-mesh strainer into a bowl. Transfer the solids in the strainer to a blender or food processor and pulse until semi-smooth. Reserve the liquid in the bowl.

5 Return the chicken to the slow cooker, along with the sauce in the blender. Sprinkle with the remaining ¾ teaspoon of salt and ½ teaspoon of cumin, and add the lime juice. If you prefer a thinner sauce, stir in some of the reserved liquid. Serve.

INGREDIENT TIP Tomatillos look like small green tomatoes with a papery husk. They provide a tomato-like flavor with a slight citrusy bite to it. They are best when firm and bright green. Don't choose fruit that looks dried out, shriveled, or blemished.

PER SERVING Calories: 205; Total Fat: 7g; Saturated Fat: 1g; Cholesterol: 127mg; Sodium: 815mg; Total Carbohydrates: 6g; Fiber: 2g; Protein: 30g

TURKEY

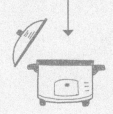

Turkey Breast and Gravy

SERVES 8 • PREP TIME: 10 MINUTES
COOK TIME: 8 HOURS

BIG 8 ALLERGEN FREE
SET AND FORGET

1 tablespoon olive oil

2 teaspoons garlic powder

½ teaspoon dried crushed rosemary

½ teaspoon dried thyme

½ teaspoon ground sage

½ teaspoon onion powder

½ teaspoon salt, plus
more for seasoning

½ teaspoon freshly ground black
pepper, plus more for seasoning

1 (4-pound) bone-in turkey breast

2 tablespoons cornstarch

2 tablespoons water

When I was a child, my favorite hot lunch at school was turkey and gravy. It was always served over a pile of mashed potatoes with green beans. I don't know how much I'd like cafeteria turkey and gravy as an adult, but I do know that I love this dish made at home in the slow cooker! Just as in the old days, I serve it with mashed potatoes and green beans.

1 In a small bowl, whisk together the olive oil, garlic powder, rosemary, thyme, sage, onion powder, salt, and pepper. Rub the oil and herb mixture all over the turkey breast. Place the turkey in the slow cooker.

2 Cover and cook on low for 8 hours, or until the temperature at the thickest part of the breast registers 165°F.

3 Transfer the turkey to a cutting board. Tent with aluminum foil and let it rest for 10 minutes.

4 While the turkey is resting, make the gravy. Carefully pour the drippings from the slow cooker through a fine-mesh strainer into a saucepan. In a small bowl, whisk together the cornstarch and water until smooth. Add the cornstarch slurry to the saucepan with the drippings. Whisk over medium-high heat, stirring often, until the mixture bubbles and thickens, about 5 minutes. Season with additional salt and pepper, if needed.

5 Slice the turkey and serve with the gravy.

INGREDIENT TIP If the turkey is frozen, make sure to allow enough time for it to thaw. A 4-pound turkey breast will need about 24 hours to thaw in the refrigerator.

PER SERVING Calories: 406; Total Fat: 18g; Saturated Fat: 4g; Cholesterol: 140mg; Sodium: 428mg; Total Carbohydrates: 3g; Fiber: 0g; Protein: 48g

Spiced Turkey Breast

SERVES 6 • PREP TIME: 10 MINUTES
COOK TIME: 8 HOURS

BIG 8 ALLERGEN FREE
SET AND FORGET

1 tablespoon olive oil

2 teaspoons smoked paprika

1 teaspoon brown sugar

1 teaspoon dried sage

½ teaspoon chili powder

½ teaspoon garlic powder

½ teaspoon onion powder

½ teaspoon salt

½ teaspoon freshly
ground black pepper

1 (2-pound) bone-in turkey
breast half, skin removed

Because this turkey is wrapped in foil while it's cooking, it stays especially moist and tender. It reminds me of how turkey turns out when it's cooked in an oven bag. It goes well with a side of corn on the cob or a cucumber salad.

1 In a small bowl, whisk together the olive oil, paprika, brown sugar, sage, chili powder, garlic powder, onion powder, salt, and pepper. Place the turkey on a large sheet of aluminum foil. Rub the oil mixture all over the turkey. Loosely wrap the turkey in the foil and place it in the slow cooker.

2 Cover and cook on low for 8 hours, or until the temperature at the thickest part of the breast registers 165°F.

3 Gently open the foil, being careful of the steam. Transfer the turkey to a cutting board. Loosely tent the turkey with foil and let it rest for 10 minutes.

4 Slice the turkey and serve.

SIMPLE SWAP If you prefer, you can use a 2-pound boneless turkey breast instead of a bone-in breast. If you opt for the boneless turkey breast, reduce the cooking time to 6 hours on low.

PER SERVING Calories: 157; Total Fat: 3g; Saturated Fat: 0g; Cholesterol: 70mg; Sodium: 252mg; Total Carbohydrates: 2g; Fiber: 1g; Protein: 28g

Turkey Meatloaf with Baked Potatoes

SERVES 4 • PREP TIME: 10 MINUTES
COOK TIME: 8 HOURS

SET AND FORGET

1 pound ground turkey

1 (8-ounce) can tomato sauce

1 cup Italian-style bread crumbs

½ cup finely diced yellow onion

1 teaspoon salt

¼ teaspoon freshly ground black pepper

4 russet potatoes

Turkey meatloaf with baked potatoes is a traditional dinner that everyone loves, but I bet you didn't know how easy it is to make in the slow cooker. I like to pair this meal with a green salad or a side of steamed green beans.

1 In a large bowl, combine the turkey, tomato sauce, bread crumbs, onion, salt, and pepper. Mix with your hands to combine thoroughly. Place the meatloaf mixture in a loaf pan that fits inside your slow cooker insert. Shape the mixture into a loaf, leaving some room between the loaf and the pan sides for melted fat to collect. Cover the top of the pan with aluminum foil. Place the pan in the slow cooker.

2 Scrub the potatoes and pierce each potato with a fork several times. Wrap the potatoes in foil. Place the potatoes around the loaf pan. You may need to stack them to fit or even balance them on the sides of the loaf pan.

3 Cover and cook on low for 8 hours.

4 Transfer the loaf pan to a wire rack, remove the foil, and let it sit for 5 minutes. Slice and serve with the baked potatoes.

TASTY TIP Because the meatloaf is cooked in the slow cooker, it won't have a chance to brown on top. I like to cover the top of the finished meatloaf with barbecue sauce and place the pan under the broiler for 3 minutes to brown the top, which will enhance the flavor and make it look even yummier.

ALLERGY TIP If you're allergic to wheat, you can replace the bread crumbs with quick-cooking rolled oats.

PER SERVING Calories: 245; Total Fat: 3g; Saturated Fat: 1g; Cholesterol: 62mg; Sodium: 1,053mg; Total Carbohydrates: 26g; Fiber: 3g; Protein: 30g

Turkey Meatballs

SERVES 4 • PREP TIME: 15 MINUTES
COOK TIME: 5 HOURS

1 pound lean ground turkey

1 large egg, lightly beaten

½ cup bread crumbs

1 teaspoon chili powder

1 teaspoon salt

½ teaspoon garlic powder

½ teaspoon onion powder

1 (28-ounce) jar all-natural or organic spaghetti sauce

1 cup shredded mozzarella cheese

Cooked spaghetti, for serving (optional)

When time is at a premium, these flavorful but nearly no-prep meatballs will fit the bill. The meatballs are cooked alongside your favorite pasta sauce and can be served with spaghetti, making this a family friendly dinner. My children especially love shredded mozzarella cheese on top of their meatballs and spaghetti.

1 In a large bowl, combine the turkey, egg, bread crumbs, chili powder, salt, garlic powder, and onion powder, and mix with clean hands to combine thoroughly. Shape the mixture into 1-inch meatballs. Place the meatballs in the slow cooker. Pour the spaghetti sauce over the meatballs.

2 Cover and cook on low for 5 hours.

3 Remove the lid and sprinkle the mozzarella cheese over the meatballs and sauce. Cook on high without the lid until the cheese is melted, about 10 minutes.

4 Carefully scoop the meatballs and sauce onto serving plates—over spaghetti, if desired.

ALLERGY TIP If you're allergic to dairy, substitute vegan cheese for the mozzarella cheese. If you're allergic to wheat, use quick-cooking rolled oats instead of the bread crumbs.

PER SERVING Calories: 311; Total Fat: 13g; Saturated Fat: 2g; Cholesterol: 115mg; Sodium: 1,336mg; Total Carbohydrates: 21g; Fiber: 3g; Protein: 27g

Turkey Tostadas

SERVES 6 • PREP TIME: 10 MINUTES
COOK TIME: 8 HOURS

**BIG 8 ALLERGEN FREE
SET AND FORGET**

**1 (2-pound) bone-in turkey
breast half, skin removed**

2 cups salsa

6 (6-inch) corn tortillas

1 avocado, peeled, pitted, and diced

2 tablespoons chopped fresh cilantro

Optional toppings: sour cream,
lime wedges, shredded cheese

These turkey tostadas make a tasty, satisfying meal. But if you're feeling very hungry, you may want to serve them with Mexican Beans and Rice (page 50).

1 Place the turkey breast, meaty side up, in the slow cooker. Pour the salsa over the turkey.

2 Cover and cook on low for 8 hours, or until the temperature at the thickest part of the breast registers 165°F.

3 Transfer the turkey to a cutting board. Let it rest for 10 minutes. Cut the turkey into ½-inch-thick slices. Using two forks, pull the meat apart into long shreds. Return the shredded turkey to the salsa in the slow cooker.

4 Put a tortilla on each serving plate. Spoon some turkey and salsa over the tortillas. Top with avocado and cilantro and your favorite toppings.

TASTY TIP To make this dish more like an authentic tostada, you may want to crisp the tortillas. Heat the oven to 425°F. While the cooked turkey is resting, lightly spray both sides of each tortilla with nonstick cooking spray. Place the tortillas in a single layer on a rimmed baking sheet. Bake the tortillas for 7 to 10 minutes, or until crisp and lightly browned on the edges.

PER SERVING Calories: 366; Total Fat: 17g; Saturated Fat: 4g;
Cholesterol: 82mg; Sodium: 696mg; Total Carbohydrates: 19g;
Fiber: 52g; Protein: 31g

Chipotle Turkey Sliders

SERVES 6 • PREP TIME: 15 MINUTES
COOK TIME: 8 HOURS

SET AND FORGET

4 pounds turkey drumsticks

1 (7-ounce) can chipotle peppers in adobo sauce

⅓ cup apple cider vinegar

12 slider buns

2 cups fresh coleslaw salad and dressing mix, mixed

Spicy chipotle peppers in adobo sauce give the turkey meat plenty of heat and flavor. If you are sensitive to spiciness, you may want to use only half a can of chipotle peppers. I love serving this turkey on Hawaiian sweet rolls for the mix of spicy and sweet flavors.

1 Put the turkey drumsticks in the slow cooker.

2 In a blender or food processor, pulse the chipotle peppers and sauce with the vinegar a few times to coarsely chop. Spread the chipotle mixture over the drumsticks.

3 Cover and cook on low for 8 hours, or until the meat falls off the bones.

4 Transfer the drumsticks to a cutting board. Discard the skin and bones and shred the meat with two forks. Mix the shredded turkey with just enough sauce to moisten (the mixture is very spicy).

5 Serve the turkey on the slider buns, topped with coleslaw.

SIMPLE SWAP You can substitute turkey thighs for the turkey drumsticks in this recipe if you wish.

ALLERGY TIP If you're allergic to wheat, use gluten-free rolls or bread in place of conventional slider buns.

PER SERVING Calories: 626; Total Fat: 28g; Saturated Fat: 7g; Cholesterol: 218mg; Sodium: 783mg; Total Carbohydrates: 31g; Fiber: 3g; Protein: 64g

Turkey Sausage-Stuffed Peppers

SERVES 4 • PREP TIME: 10 MINUTES
COOK TIME: 5 HOURS

1 pound lean ground turkey sausage

1 (10-ounce) can diced
tomatoes with green chiles

1 cup frozen cooked brown rice

1 teaspoon garlic powder

1½ cups shredded sharp
Cheddar cheese, divided

4 bell peppers (any color)

¼ cup water

Salt

Freshly ground black pepper

This recipe uses ground turkey sausage to accompany the rice and peppers. The turkey sausage has herbs and spices in it, which add flavor to the dish. If you're having a hard time finding turkey sausage in the meat department at your grocery store, look in the breakfast section of the frozen foods aisle.

1 In a large bowl, stir together the sausage, tomatoes with their juice, brown rice, garlic powder, and 1 cup of Cheddar cheese.

2 Cut off the top of each pepper. Remove the ribs and seeds. Stuff the sausage mixture into the peppers.

3 Pour the water into the slow cooker. Place the stuffed peppers standing upright in the slow cooker. Lean them against each other if they need support.

4 Cover and cook on low for 5 hours.

5 Season with salt and pepper. Sprinkle the remaining ½ cup of cheese on top of the peppers and let it melt. Serve hot.

ALLERGY TIP If you are allergic to dairy, substitute a vegan cheese for the Cheddar.

PER SERVING Calories: 386; Total Fat: 22g; Saturated Fat: 11g; Cholesterol: 100mg; Sodium: 1,003mg; Total Carbohydrates: 23g; Fiber: 3g; Protein: 27g

Turkey Cassoulet

SERVES 4 • PREP TIME: 15 MINUTES
COOK TIME: 8 HOURS

BIG 8 ALLERGEN FREE
SET AND FORGET

1 (15-ounce) can cannellini beans, rinsed and drained

1 pound turkey kielbasa, cut into ½-inch rounds

1 red bell pepper, seeded and chopped

1 large leek, trimmed and sliced

1 cup chicken broth

½ teaspoon dried thyme

¼ teaspoon salt, plus more for seasoning

¼ teaspoon freshly ground black pepper, plus more for seasoning

⅓ cup chopped fresh parsley, for garnish

Traditional cassoulet is a rich, slow-cooked casserole originating in the south of France, containing meat, pork, and white beans. In this version, I use turkey kielbasa and cannellini beans simmered in a flavorful sauce for a delicious weeknight meal. I like to serve this dish with some leafy greens.

1 Combine the beans, turkey kielbasa, red bell pepper, leek, broth, thyme, salt, and pepper in the slow cooker and stir to combine.

2 Cover and cook on low for 8 hours.

3 Using a slotted spoon, transfer the beans and turkey to a serving platter. Discard the cooking liquid. Season with additional salt and pepper, if needed. Garnish with the parsley and serve.

INGREDIENT TIP Leeks add a distinctive flavor to any dish, but they can get really sandy between the leaves while they grow. To rinse them well, cut the leek into ¼-inch slices; discard the root. Fill a bowl with cold water. Place the sliced leeks in the water and swirl them around, letting the sand and dirt sink to the bottom of the bowl. Skim the top of the surface with your hand to pick up the floating leeks. Dry them on paper towels or a clean dish towel.

PER SERVING Calories: 261; Total Fat: 7g; Saturated Fat: 3g; Cholesterol: 28mg; Sodium: 1,236mg; Total Carbohydrates: 28g; Fiber: 8g; Protein: 27g

Creamy Ground Turkey and Mushrooms

SERVES 4 • PREP TIME: 10 MINUTES
COOK TIME: 5 HOURS

1 pound ground turkey

1 pound white mushrooms, sliced

½ cup beef broth

½ teaspoon onion powder

½ teaspoon garlic powder

¼ teaspoon dried thyme

¾ teaspoon salt, plus
more for seasoning

¼ teaspoon freshly ground black
pepper, plus more for seasoning

½ cup sour cream

¼ cup chopped scallions

Sometimes we serve this turkey and mushroom dish over egg noodles or rice. If you want to prepare a low-carb version, you can eliminate the sour cream and wrap the turkey and mushroom mixture in crisp lettuce leaves for a lettuce wrap.

1 Put the ground turkey in the slow cooker, and break up the turkey into chunks with a wooden spoon. Add the mushrooms, beef broth, onion powder, garlic powder, thyme, salt, and pepper. Stir to combine.

2 Cover and cook on low for 5 hours. Remove the lid and break up the turkey into smaller pieces with a wooden spoon. Stir in the sour cream and scallions. Season with additional salt and pepper, if needed, and serve.

SIMPLE SWAP   You can replace the sour cream with plain yogurt or 4 ounces of softened cream cheese, if you wish.

ALLERGY TIP   If you are allergic to dairy, omit the sour cream.

PER SERVING Calories: 220; Total Fat: 9g; Saturated Fat: 4g; Cholesterol: 75mg; Sodium: 613mg; Total Carbohydrates: 6g; Fiber: 1g; Protein: 32g

Sesame-Sriracha Turkey Lettuce Wraps

SERVES 8 • PREP TIME: 10 MINUTES
COOK TIME: 5 HOURS

BIG 8 ALLERGEN FREE

2 pounds lean ground turkey

2 tablespoons grated fresh ginger

2 tablespoons Sriracha sauce,
plus more for serving

2 tablespoons toasted sesame seeds

2 teaspoons garlic powder

1½ teaspoons salt

8 large lettuce leaves, for serving

Sriracha sauce is a hot chili sauce from Thailand. It's made from a paste of hot chiles, distilled vinegar, garlic, sugar, and salt. Its popularity has boomed in the past few years, and you can find everything from Sriracha potato chips to Sriracha beef jerky. I love the cool crispness of lettuce leaves paired with the spicy turkey meat.

1 Put the ground turkey in the slow cooker and break up the meat into chunks with a wooden spoon. Add the ginger, Sriracha, sesame seeds, garlic powder, and salt and stir to combine.

2 Cover and cook on low for 5 hours.

3 Break up the meat into smaller pieces with a wooden spoon and stir. Serve the meat wrapped up in the lettuce leaves and top with extra Sriracha, if desired.

INGREDIENT TIP Sriracha sauce adds lots of heat, so if you prefer less spice, you can halve the amount called for.

PER SERVING Calories: 144; Total Fat: 2g; Saturated Fat: 0g; Cholesterol: 55mg; Sodium: 1,742mg; Total Carbohydrates: 4g; Fiber: 1g; Protein: 29g

Chapter

8

BEEF

Pot Roast

SERVES 6 • PREP TIME: 10 MINUTES
COOK TIME: 8 HOURS

**BIG 8 ALLERGEN FREE
SET AND FORGET**

2 pounds beef chuck roast,
trimmed of excess fat

1 pound russet potatoes,
peeled and quartered

1 pound baby carrots

1 medium yellow onion, quartered

1 tablespoon steak seasoning

½ cup beef broth

Salt

Freshly ground black pepper

Pot roast is one of those comforting, old-fashioned meals that remind me of Sunday dinner at Grandma's house. The best cut of beef to cook low and slow is beef chuck roast. Over many hours, it becomes fork tender. If the beef isn't tender, you haven't cooked it long enough!

1 Cut the roast into 4 equal pieces. Arrange the beef, potatoes, carrots, and onion in the slow cooker. Sprinkle the beef and vegetables with the steak seasoning. Pour in the broth.

2 Cover and cook on low for 8 hours, or until the beef and vegetables are tender.

3 Transfer the beef to a cutting board. Slice the beef and put it in a serving dish, along with the vegetables and the juices from the slow cooker. Season with salt and pepper, if needed.

SIMPLE SWAP If you would like to substitute sweet potatoes for russets, you can use peeled sweet potatoes cut into large chunks.

INGREDIENT TIP It's easy to make a batch of your own steak seasoning from scratch. In a small bowl, combine 2 tablespoons kosher salt, 2 tablespoons freshly ground black pepper, 2 tablespoons paprika, 1 tablespoon granulated garlic, 1 tablespoon onion powder, 1 tablespoon ground coriander, 1 tablespoon dried dill, and 1 tablespoon crushed red pepper flakes, and mix well. Store in an airtight glass container in a cool, dry place. This steak seasoning will stay fresh for up to 1 year.

PER SERVING Calories: 313; Total Fat: 11g; Saturated Fat: 3g; Cholesterol: 93mg; Sodium: 255mg; Total Carbohydrates: 19g; Fiber: 4g; Protein: 33g

Barbecued Beef Sandwiches

SERVES 6 • PREP TIME: 10 MINUTES
COOK TIME: 8 HOURS

SET AND FORGET

2 pounds beef chuck roast, trimmed of excess fat

1½ tablespoons brown sugar

1½ teaspoons chili powder

½ teaspoon smoked paprika

½ teaspoon ground cumin

½ teaspoon salt

¼ teaspoon freshly ground black pepper

¼ cup apple cider vinegar

¼ cup ketchup

6 buns, toasted

These barbecued beef sandwiches are a perfect dish to make for an easy summer meal. You can also serve this tasty meat over salad, on pizza, or in tacos. If you like your barbecued beef extra saucy, just double the apple cider vinegar and ketchup in the recipe.

1 Put the beef in the slow cooker. In a small bowl, combine the brown sugar, chili powder, paprika, cumin, salt, and pepper. Rub the seasoning all over the beef.

2 In a small bowl, whisk together the apple cider vinegar and ketchup and pour it over the meat.

3 Cover and cook on low for 8 hours, or until the beef is extremely tender.

4 Transfer the beef to a cutting board. With two forks, shred the beef. Stir the shredded beef back into the sauce in the slow cooker.

5 To serve, use tongs to pile the saucy beef onto the toasted buns.

TASTY TIP To make this recipe even tastier, put the beef on a large piece of aluminum foil and rub it with the seasoning mixture. Then wrap the beef tightly in the foil, put it in a baking pan, and let it sit in the refrigerator overnight before cooking it the next day.

ALLERGY TIP If you're allergic to wheat, use buns that are gluten-free or serve the beef over salad or on corn tortillas.

PER SERVING Calories: 418; Total Fat: 13g; Saturated Fat: 4g; Cholesterol: 93mg; Sodium: 723mg; Total Carbohydrates: 36g; Fiber: 2g; Protein: 37g

Beef Brisket

SERVES 8 • PREP TIME: 15 MINUTES
COOK TIME: 10 HOURS

BIG 8 ALLERGEN FREE
SET AND FORGET

1 (5-pound) beef brisket, trimmed of excess fat

2 teaspoons garlic powder

2 teaspoons chili powder

2 teaspoons salt

½ teaspoon freshly ground black pepper

½ cup ketchup

⅓ cup apple cider vinegar

2 tablespoons Worcestershire sauce

2 teaspoons Dijon mustard

¼ cup (packed) brown sugar

1 teaspoon garlic powder

Beef brisket is a cut of meat that needs to cook for a long time on low. And the longer it cooks, the more tender it becomes. This slow cooker recipe is incredibly flavorful! Enjoy the brisket as is or stack it in sandwiches.

1 Put the brisket in the slow cooker.

2 In a small bowl, combine the garlic powder, chili powder, salt, and pepper. Rub the seasoning mixture all over the brisket.

3 In a medium bowl, whisk together the ketchup, apple cider vinegar, Worcestershire sauce, Dijon mustard, brown sugar, and garlic powder. Pour the sauce over the brisket.

4 Cover and cook on low for 10 hours.

5 Transfer the brisket to a cutting board. Cut in thin slices across the grain. Return the brisket to the slow cooker and stir it into the sauce. Serve.

TASTY TIP To really pump up the flavor of this beef brisket, take the time to sear it before adding it to the slow cooker. Heat a large oiled skillet over medium-high heat with your oven fan turned on. Sear the brisket on both sides until a golden brown crust appears.

PER SERVING Calories: 818; Total Fat: 63g; Saturated Fat: 25g; Cholesterol: 225mg; Sodium: 987mg; Total Carbohydrates: 10g; Fiber: 0g; Protein: 53g

Beef Short Ribs

SERVES 6 • PREP TIME: 5 MINUTES
COOK TIME: 8 HOURS

BIG 8 ALLERGEN FREE
SET AND FORGET

2 pounds beef short ribs

4 teaspoons barbecue seasoning

2 cups barbecue sauce, divided

Tender beef short ribs were meant for long, slow cooking, so the slow cooker is an ideal cooking method for them. Look for shorter lengths, but you can use longer ribs and even boneless short ribs if that's all you can find.

1 Put the short ribs in the slow cooker. Rub them with the barbecue seasoning. Pour 1 cup of barbecue sauce over the ribs.

2 Cover and cook on low for 8 hours.

3 Serve the ribs with the remaining barbecue sauce.

INGREDIENT TIP You'll find barbecue seasoning in the spice aisle of your supermarket, but you can also make your own. Just stir together ½ cup brown sugar, ½ cup paprika, 1 tablespoon chili powder, 1 tablespoon garlic powder, 1 tablespoon onion powder, 1 tablespoon salt, 1 tablespoon freshly ground black pepper, and 1 teaspoon cayenne pepper. Store the leftovers in an airtight container in a cool, dry place.

TASTY TIP To maximize the ribs' flavor after they have cooked in the slow cooker all day, turn on your broiler. Put the cooked ribs on a rimmed baking sheet. Baste with a bit of barbecue sauce and broil for 3 minutes.

PER SERVING Calories: 712; Total Fat: 55g; Saturated Fat: 24g; Cholesterol: 113mg; Sodium: 1,007mg; Total Carbohydrates: 30g; Fiber: 1g; Protein: 21g

Sloppy Joes

SERVES 8 • PREP TIME: 10 MINUTES
COOK TIME: 8 HOURS

BIG 8 ALLERGEN FREE
SET AND FORGET

2 pounds lean ground beef

½ cup finely diced onion

½ cup chopped green bell pepper

1½ cups ketchup

2 teaspoons yellow mustard

2 tablespoons brown sugar

1 teaspoon garlic powder

Salt

Freshly ground black pepper

Sloppy Joes can feed a crowd, making it a perfect dish for a potluck or cookout. Ladle the meat over toasted hamburger buns, and serve with a side of coleslaw and a slice of watermelon.

1 Put the ground beef in the slow cooker and break up the meat with a wooden spoon. Add the onion, green bell pepper, ketchup, mustard, brown sugar, and garlic powder, and stir to combine.

2 Cover and cook on low for 8 hours. Season with salt and pepper and serve.

SUPER EASY You can buy sautéed onions in the frozen foods aisle of your grocery store. They come in cubes and are perfect for popping into the slow cooker to add flavor to meals like this. Instead of chopping and dicing (and tearing up over) raw onions, just stir one of these packages of onion cubes into the slow cooker.

PER SERVING Calories: 259; Total Fat: 10g; Saturated Fat: 5g; Cholesterol: 75mg; Sodium: 611mg; Total Carbohydrates: 15g; Fiber: 1g; Protein: 24g

French Dip Sandwiches

SERVES 6 • PREP TIME: 10 MINUTES
COOK TIME: 8 HOURS

SET AND FORGET

1 (2-pound) beef chuck roast, trimmed of excess fat

½ teaspoon salt, plus more for seasoning

¼ teaspoon freshly ground black pepper, plus more for seasoning

3 cups beef broth

¼ cup Worcestershire sauce

2 large yellow onions, very thinly sliced

2 teaspoons garlic powder

1 bay leaf

6 large crusty French rolls, toasted if desired

8 slices provolone cheese (optional)

The French dip sandwich features tender, thin slices of beef layered in a long French roll, then dipped into a flavorful sauce made from the beef juices in the roasting pan. It is a staple at any diner in America.

1 Put the beef in the slow cooker. Sprinkle with the salt and pepper. Add the broth, Worcestershire sauce, onions, garlic powder, and bay leaf.

2 Cover and cook on low for 8 hours, or until the beef is very tender.

3 Transfer the beef to a cutting board. Slice or shred the meat. Season with additional salt and pepper, if needed.

4 Place a fine-mesh strainer over a large bowl and carefully pour the juices from the slow cooker through the strainer and into the bowl. This juice will be the "au jus," or dipping sauce. Reserve the onions in the strainer and discard the bay leaf.

5 Pile the meat on the bottoms of the rolls and add some onions on top of the meat. Place a slice of cheese on top of the onions, if desired.

6 Serve the sandwiches with a small bowl of the reserved dipping sauce.

TASTY TIP For a more developed meaty flavor, you can brown the roast before adding it to the slow cooker. In a large skillet, heat 2 tablespoons of canola oil over medium-high heat. Add the meat and sear to get a brown crust on all sides.

ALLERGY TIP If you are allergic to dairy, use a vegan cheese instead of the provolone cheese or omit it. If you have a wheat allergy, you can replace the French rolls with gluten-free rolls or bread.

PER SERVING Calories: 446; Total Fat: 14g; Saturated Fat: 4g; Cholesterol: 93mg; Sodium: 1,098mg; Total Carbohydrates: 40g; Fiber: 3g; Protein: 40g

Swiss Steak

SERVES 6 • PREP TIME: 10 MINUTES
COOK TIME: 9 HOURS

SET AND FORGET

½ cup chicken broth

2 medium yellow onions, halved and thinly sliced

1 (14.5-ounce) can petite diced tomatoes

1½ pounds white mushrooms, sliced

1 teaspoon dried thyme

6 (6- to 8-ounce) beef blade steaks

½ teaspoon salt, plus more for seasoning

¼ teaspoon freshly ground black pepper, plus more for seasoning

⅓ cup heavy cream

2 tablespoons minced fresh parsley (optional)

Chuck blade steaks have a luxurious flavor at a bargain price. They are also called flat iron steaks. They're easy to spot! Just look for ovals that are slightly larger than your palm and about 1 inch thick. These steaks are cooked for hours at a low temperature for maximum tenderness. Serve the beef and sauce over wide egg noodles or garlic mashed potatoes.

1 Combine the broth, onions, tomatoes with their juice, mushrooms, and thyme in the slow cooker. Place the beef on top of the vegetables. Sprinkle with the salt and pepper.

2 Cover and cook on low for 9 hours, or until the beef is tender.

3 Transfer the steaks to a platter and tent them loosely with aluminum foil. Let the liquid in the slow cooker settle for 5 minutes, then skim off and discard the extra fat from the surface using a large spoon. Stir in the cream and parsley (if using), and season with additional salt and pepper, if desired.

4 Serve the steaks with the sauce.

SUPER EASY Buy cleaned, presliced mushrooms at the supermarket to make this recipe even easier.

ALLERGY TIP If you're allergic to dairy, substitute puréed tofu for the heavy cream. You can purée the tofu in the blender or food processor.

PER SERVING Calories: 466; Total Fat: 23g; Saturated Fat: 2g; Cholesterol: 9mg; Sodium: 341mg; Total Carbohydrates: 9g; Fiber: 2g; Protein: 54g

Beef Gyros

SERVES 4 TO 6 • PREP TIME: 10 MINUTES
COOK TIME: 8 HOURS

SET AND FORGET

**2 pounds beef chuck roast,
cut into ¼-inch strips**

1 large onion, halved and thinly sliced

¼ cup olive oil

2 tablespoons fresh lemon juice

2 teaspoons garlic powder

1 teaspoon dried oregano

½ teaspoon salt, plus
more for seasoning

¼ teaspoon freshly ground black
pepper, plus more for seasoning

Pita breads, warmed, for serving

Tzatziki sauce, for serving

Chopped lettuce and diced
tomatoes, for topping (optional)

Whether you say "yee-ro," "jai-ro," "gear-o," or "hero," gyros are tasty, popular Greek American sandwiches that you don't need to be able to pronounce to enjoy. Thinly sliced seasoned lamb, beef, or chicken is placed in a pita and topped with refreshing tzatziki sauce.

1 Combine the beef and onion in the slow cooker.

2 In a small bowl, whisk together the olive oil, lemon juice, garlic powder, oregano, salt, and pepper. Pour the dressing over the meat and toss to coat.

3 Cover and cook on low for 8 hours, or until the beef is tender.

4 Season with additional salt and pepper, if needed. Serve the beef and onions in pitas with tzatziki sauce, topped with lettuce and tomatoes if desired.

INGREDIENT TIP You can easily make your own tzatziki sauce. Just stir together 1 cup plain Greek yogurt, 1 tablespoon fresh lemon juice, 1 seeded and diced cucumber, 1 minced garlic clove, 1 tablespoon dried dill, and plenty of salt and pepper. Store the leftover sauce in an airtight glass container in the refrigerator for up to 3 days.

ALLERGY TIP If you're allergic to dairy, forgo the tzatziki sauce. If you're allergic to wheat, you can serve the meat in a salad or use gluten-free pita.

PER SERVING Calories: 553; Total Fat: 30g; Saturated Fat: 7g; Cholesterol: 140mg; Sodium: 605mg; Total Carbohydrates: 21g; Fiber: 2g; Protein: 49g

Korean Beef

SERVES 6 • PREP TIME: 5 MINUTES
COOK TIME: 7 HOURS

BIG 8 ALLERGEN FREE

2 pounds extra-lean ground beef

⅓ cup tamari or low-sodium soy sauce

2 tablespoons toasted sesame oil

2 tablespoons tomato paste

2 teaspoons minced fresh ginger

½ cup (packed) brown sugar

2 teaspoons garlic powder

½ teaspoon red pepper flakes

Chopped scallions, for
garnish (optional)

With the bold flavors of tamari, sesame oil, and ginger in this dish, you won't even notice that the beef hasn't been browned. This is a super simple version of Korean beef and is perfect served in lettuce wraps or on top of brown rice.

1 Put the beef in the slow cooker and break it up with a wooden spoon.

2 In a small bowl, whisk together the tamari, sesame oil, tomato paste, ginger, brown sugar, garlic powder, and red pepper flakes. Stir the mixture into the beef to coat it.

3 Cover and cook on low for 7 hours.

4 Stir the beef mixture again, breaking it up into smaller chunks. Garnish with scallions (if using) and serve.

SIMPLE SWAP You can use lean ground turkey in place of ground beef if you wish. Reduce the cooking time to 4 hours on low.

PER SERVING Calories: 372; Total Fat: 18g; Saturated Fat: 7g; Cholesterol: 100mg; Sodium: 1,003mg; Total Carbohydrates: 15g; Fiber: 1g; Protein: 33g

Beef and Broccoli

SERVES 4 • PREP TIME: 10 MINUTES
COOK TIME: 8 HOURS

Beef and broccoli is one of my favorite dishes to order when we go to a Chinese restaurant. This recipe tastes just as good when it is made at home in your slow cooker.

SET AND FORGET

1 (1½-pound) beef chuck roast, cut into ¼-inch strips

½ cup tamari or low-sodium soy sauce

2 tablespoons toasted sesame oil

⅓ cup brown sugar

1 teaspoon garlic powder

2 tablespoons cornstarch

2 tablespoons water

1 (1-pound) bag frozen broccoli florets

Steamed rice, for serving (optional)

1 Put the beef strips in the slow cooker.

2 In a small bowl, whisk together the tamari, sesame oil, brown sugar, and garlic powder. Pour the mixture over the beef.

3 Cover and cook on low for 8 hours.

4 In a small bowl, whisk together the cornstarch and water. Stir the cornstarch slurry into the slow cooker. Turn to high and let the sauce thicken, stirring frequently, with the lid off.

5 Pour the broccoli florets into a colander. Run hot water over the broccoli until it's thawed. Shake the colander to release any extra water. Stir the broccoli into the meat mixture and cook for 3 minutes to heat through.

6 Serve the beef and broccoli with rice, if desired.

SIMPLE SWAP Tamari can be found in the Asian aisle of your grocery store. It is similar to soy sauce, but thicker. If you can't find tamari, you can substitute low-sodium soy sauce.

PER SERVING Calories: 414; Total Fat: 19g; Saturated Fat: 5g; Cholesterol: 105mg; Sodium: 2,154mg; Total Carbohydrates: 20g; Fiber: 4g; Protein: 42g

Massaman Beef Curry

SERVES 6 • PREP TIME: 10 MINUTES
COOK TIME: 8 HOURS

SET AND FORGET

1 (13.5-ounce) can coconut milk

⅓ cup chunky all-natural peanut butter

3 tablespoons Thai red curry paste

2 tablespoons fresh lime juice

2 tablespoons (packed) brown sugar

½ teaspoon ground ginger

½ teaspoon garlic powder

1 (1½-pound) beef chuck roast, trimmed of excess fat and cut into bite-size pieces

2 tablespoons cornstarch

2 tablespoons water

Massaman curry is a rich, relatively mild Thai curry that is an interpretation of a Persian dish. It has a strong peanut flavor thanks to the generous portion of peanut butter. This is a pared-down version of massaman for the slow cooker, and it tastes wonderful served over boiled potatoes or rice.

1 Combine the coconut milk, peanut butter, curry paste, lime juice, brown sugar, ginger, and garlic powder in the slow cooker. Whisk until smooth. Stir in the beef.

2 Cover and cook on low for 8 hours.

3 In a small bowl, whisk together the cornstarch and water. Stir the cornstarch slurry into the slow cooker. Turn to high and let the sauce thicken, stirring occasionally, without the lid. Serve.

SUPER EASY To make this recipe even easier, instead of cutting and trimming the beef chuck roast, buy a package of ready-to-go beef stew meat.

ALLERGY TIP If anyone coming to dinner is allergic to peanuts, omit the peanut butter. If you aren't allergic to almonds, you can replace the peanut butter with almond butter.

PER SERVING Calories: 578; Total Fat: 43g; Saturated Fat: 20g; Cholesterol: 70mg; Sodium: 477mg; Total Carbohydrates: 19g; Fiber: 5g; Protein: 34g

Shredded Beef Tacos

SERVES 6 • PREP TIME: 15 MINUTES
COOK TIME: 8 HOURS

¼ cup beef broth

¼ cup fresh lime juice

2 tablespoons tomato paste

1 teaspoon ground cumin

1 teaspoon smoked paprika

1 teaspoon salt

½ teaspoon freshly
ground black pepper

½ teaspoon garlic powder

1 medium yellow onion, finely diced

1 jalapeño pepper, seeded
and minced (optional)

1 (2-pound) beef chuck roast,
trimmed of excess fat

Large flour tortillas, for serving

Optional toppings: shredded cheese,
sour cream, chopped tomatoes,
chopped lettuce, chopped fresh cilantro

For this shredded beef tacos recipe, I use my favorite cut of beef for the slow cooker, beef chuck roast. If you can't find beef chuck in your supermarket, you can use cross rib roast instead.

1 Combine the broth, lime juice, tomato paste, cumin, paprika, salt, pepper, and garlic powder in the slow cooker. Whisk until smooth. Stir in the onion and jalapeño (if using). Add the roast.

2 Cover and cook on low for 8 hours, or until the beef is tender.

3 Transfer the beef to a cutting board and shred the beef with two forks. Return the beef to the slow cooker and stir it in with the juices. Serve the beef on tortillas, and top with your favorite taco toppings.

ALLERGY TIP If you are allergic to wheat, you can use gluten-free tortillas.

PER SERVING Calories: 300; Total Fat: 12g; Saturated Fat: 4g; Cholesterol: 93mg; Sodium: 537mg; Total Carbohydrates: 16g; Fiber: 3g; Protein: 33g

Flank Steak Fajitas

SERVES 5 • PREP TIME: 15 MINUTES
COOK TIME: 8 HOURS

SET AND FORGET

2 medium yellow onions, halved and thinly sliced

2 teaspoons olive oil

2 bell peppers (any color), seeded and sliced lengthwise

1 cup salsa

1 (1½-pound) flank steak, trimmed of excess fat

1 teaspoon ground cumin

1 teaspoon chili powder

½ teaspoon garlic powder

½ teaspoon onion powder

½ teaspoon salt

¼ teaspoon freshly ground black pepper

5 (8-inch) flour tortillas

Optional toppings: shredded cheese, sour cream, guacamole, pico de gallo, chopped fresh cilantro

Few foods are better than Mexican food topped generously with guacamole. I could eat it every day of my life. These fajitas use flank steak, a less expensive cut of meat than skirt steak, which is traditionally used in fajitas. It gets juicy and tender in the slow cooker.

1 Put the onions in the slow cooker. Drizzle with the olive oil. Add the bell peppers. Pour the salsa over the peppers and onions.

2 Place the steak on top of the peppers and onions. Sprinkle the steak with the cumin, chili powder, garlic powder, onion powder, salt, and pepper.

3 Cover and cook on low for 8 hours.

4 Transfer the beef to a cutting board. Tent the beef loosely with aluminum foil and let it sit for 10 minutes. Slice into thin strips.

5 Serve the beef on top of the tortillas, and use a slotted spoon to spoon the onions and bell peppers over the beef. Serve with any toppings you like.

SIMPLE SWAP If you don't want to measure out all those spices, just use 1 tablespoon of premade fajita seasoning mix instead. Or make a double recipe of the seasoning, and store the extra in an airtight container in a dark cupboard so it will be ready the next time you make this recipe.

PER SERVING Calories: 412; Total Fat: 14g; Saturated Fat: 5g; Cholesterol: 60mg; Sodium: 1,032mg; Total Carbohydrates: 36g; Fiber: 4g; Protein: 36g

Picadillo Beef

SERVES 8 • PREP TIME: 10 MINUTES
COOK TIME: 8 HOURS

**BIG 8 ALLERGEN FREE
SET AND FORGET**

8 ounces lean ground beef

1 (14.5-ounce) can diced tomatoes
with green pepper, celery, and onion

2 tablespoons tomato paste

¼ cup alcaparrado or
diced green olives

2 teaspoons garlic powder

1½ teaspoons ground cumin

½ teaspoon salt, plus
more for seasoning

¼ teaspoon freshly ground black
pepper, plus more for seasoning

2 bay leaves

¼ cup chopped fresh cilantro

Picadillo, a flavorful Cuban dish, is a perfect week-night meal. It's made with ground beef and a sauce of simmered tomatoes, green olives, bell peppers, and cumin. It is particularly good served over hot rice.

1 Put the ground beef in the slow cooker and break it up with a wooden spoon. Add the tomatoes with their juice, tomato paste, alcaparrado, garlic powder, cumin, salt, pepper, and bay leaves. Stir to combine.

2 Cover and cook on low for 8 hours.

3 Discard the bay leaves. Stir in the cilantro. Season with additional salt and pepper, if desired, and serve.

INGREDIENT TIP *Alcaparrado* is a Spanish mixture of green olives and capers. Sometimes the olives are stuffed with pimientos. To really add flavor to this beef, pour a couple of tablespoons of the juice from the jar into the dish as you are making it.

PER SERVING Calories: 82; Total Fat: 4g; Saturated Fat: 1g; Cholesterol: 19mg; Sodium: 310mg; Total Carbohydrates: 5g; Fiber: 1g; Protein: 7g

Chapter

9

PORK & LAMB

Smoky Pulled Pork

SERVES 6 • PREP TIME: 10 MINUTES
COOK TIME: 9 HOURS

BIG 8 ALLERGEN FREE
SET AND FORGET

1 (2-pound) pork shoulder (also known as Boston butt), trimmed of excess fat

½ cup chicken broth

1 tablespoon tamari or low-sodium soy sauce

1 tablespoon liquid smoke

1 garlic clove, minced

If you love smoky pulled pork but you don't have a smoker, you're going to love this easy slow cooker recipe. I like to serve this meat on a toasted bun with coleslaw.

1 Cut the pork roast into four even pieces and put them in the slow cooker. Pour the broth, soy sauce, liquid smoke, and garlic over the pork.

2 Cover and cook on low for 9 hours.

3 Transfer the pork to a carving board and shred the meat. Serve.

SIMPLE SWAP If you don't have fresh garlic on hand, you can use ½ teaspoon of garlic powder in place of the minced garlic.

PER SERVING Calories: 392; Total Fat: 31g; Saturated Fat: 11g; Cholesterol: 107mg; Sodium: 331mg; Total Carbohydrates: 0g; Fiber: 0g; Protein: 26g

St. Louis-Style Ribs

SERVES 4 • PREP TIME: 10 MINUTES
COOK TIME: 8 HOURS

BIG 8 ALLERGEN FREE
SET AND FORGET

1 (2½-pound) rack
St. Louis–style pork ribs

2½ teaspoons barbecue seasoning

1 cup water

½ cup **barbecue sauce**

These are without a doubt the best (and easiest) ribs that you can make at home. After slow cooking all day, the meat practically falls off the bone. This is one of my husband's favorite meals. We like to serve ribs with baked potatoes and a side salad.

1 Rub the rack of ribs with the barbecue seasoning and put it in the slow cooker. Coil the ribs around the walls of the slow cooker with the meaty side facing out. Pour the water into the slow cooker.

2 Cover and cook on low for 8 hours.

3 Spoon the barbecue sauce over the top of the ribs and serve.

TASTY TIP To make the ribs even more tantalizing, place them on a rimmed baking sheet after adding the barbecue sauce and brown them under the broiler for 3 minutes.

PER SERVING Calories: 547; Total Fat: 33g; Saturated Fat: 13g; Cholesterol: 113mg; Sodium: 1,037mg; Total Carbohydrates: 11g; Fiber: 0g; Protein: 50g

Mexican Pulled Pork

SERVES 6 • PREP TIME: 10 MINUTES
COOK TIME: 9 HOURS

BIG 8 ALLERGEN FREE
SET AND FORGET

1 large yellow onion, cut into thick slices

1 cup chicken broth

1 (2-pound) pork shoulder (also known as Boston butt), trimmed of excess fat

1 (14.5-ounce) can diced tomatoes with jalapeños

1 tablespoon tomato paste

¾ teaspoon garlic salt

½ teaspoon dried oregano

Salt

Freshly ground black pepper

This recipe makes perfect fall-apart-tender pork, with just a few added ingredients to give the meat a Southwestern flair. The pork is delicious for tacos, salads, nachos, and burritos!

1 Put the onion slices in the slow cooker. Pour in the broth. Place the pork on top of the onions.

2 Cover and cook on low for 9 hours, or until the meat is very tender.

3 Transfer the pork to a cutting board and shred the meat with two forks. Discard the onions and liquid in the slow cooker. Return the meat to the slow cooker.

4 Turn the slow cooker to high. Add the tomatoes with their juice, tomato paste, garlic salt, and oregano. Stir the meat until evenly coated. Cover and cook for a few minutes, until heated through. Season with salt and pepper and serve.

SIMPLE SWAP If you can't find canned diced tomatoes with jalapeños, you can substitute a can of fire-roasted salsa-style diced tomatoes plus a 4-ounce can of chopped jalapeños.

PER SERVING Calories: 417; Total Fat: 31g; Saturated Fat: 11g; Cholesterol: 107mg; Sodium: 386mg; Total Carbohydrates: 6g; Fiber: 1g; Protein: 27g

Pork and Broccoli

SERVES 6 • PREP TIME: 10 MINUTES
COOK TIME: 8 HOURS

**BIG 8 ALLERGEN FREE
SET AND FORGET**

1 cup beef broth

¼ **cup tamari or low-sodium soy sauce**

¼ **cup oyster sauce**

1 **teaspoon toasted sesame oil**

¼ cup (packed) brown sugar

1 teaspoon garlic powder

2 **pounds pork stew meat**

¼ cup cornstarch

¼ cup water

1 **(16-ounce) package frozen broccoli**

This recipe is inspired by the flavors of Chinese-style beef and broccoli but uses pork instead. Tender pieces of pork and a super savory sauce with broccoli all go together nicely over steamed white rice.

1 Combine the beef broth, tamari, oyster sauce, sesame oil, brown sugar, and garlic powder in the slow cooker. Whisk until smooth. Add the pork and stir to coat with the sauce.

2 Cover and cook on low for 8 hours.

3 Remove the lid and turn to high. Make a slurry by whisking together the cornstarch and water in a small bowl. Add the slurry to the slow cooker and stir well; the liquid should thicken a bit.

4 Put the frozen broccoli in a colander and run hot water over it until it's warmed through. Shake off the excess liquid. Stir the broccoli into the slow cooker. Let the sauce thicken for 10 minutes before serving.

SIMPLE SWAP You can use steamed fresh broccoli in place of frozen broccoli in this recipe.

PER SERVING Calories: 319; Total Fat: 12g; Saturated Fat: 4g; Cholesterol: 100mg; Sodium: 1,011mg; Total Carbohydrates: 17g; Fiber: 2g; Protein: 34g

Cilantro-Lime Shredded Pork

SERVES 6 TO 8 • PREP TIME: 5 MINUTES
COOK TIME: 8 HOURS

BIG 8 ALLERGEN FREE
SET AND FORGET

2½ pounds country-style pork ribs, trimmed of excess fat

¼ cup fresh lime juice

1 tablespoon chili powder

1 tablespoon ground cumin

2 teaspoons salt

½ cup chopped fresh cilantro

This zesty, versatile shredded pork can be served over salads or in tacos, burritos, quesadillas, or enchiladas. This dish is a perfect kid-friendly summer meal.

1 Put the pork in the slow cooker. Pour the lime juice over the pork and sprinkle with the chili powder, cumin, and salt.

2 Cover and cook on low for 8 hours.

3 Transfer the pork to a cutting board and shred the meat with two forks. Return the pork to the slow cooker and stir. Add the chopped cilantro and serve.

RECIPE TIP Prep this recipe ahead of time as a slow cooker freezer meal. Just combine all the ingredients in a gallon-size resealable plastic bag and freeze. The day before you want to cook the meal, remove the bag from the freezer and let it thaw in the fridge overnight. Dump everything into the slow cooker, cover, and cook on low for 8 hours.

PER SERVING Calories: 360; Total Fat: 22g; Saturated Fat: 8g; Cholesterol: 142mg; Sodium: 907mg; Total Carbohydrates: 2g; Fiber: 1g; Protein: 37g

Smothered Pork Chops

SERVES 4 • PREP TIME: 10 MINUTES
COOK TIME: 4 HOURS

½ cup finely diced onion

5 slices cooked bacon, crumbled, divided

½ cup chicken broth

2 teaspoons tamari or low-sodium soy sauce

¼ cup flour

1 teaspoon garlic powder

½ teaspoon dried thyme

½ teaspoon brown sugar

1 bay leaf

4 bone-in pork chops

Salt

Freshly ground black pepper

1½ teaspoons apple cider vinegar

This flavorful dish is one we like to serve in mid-summer with a side of mashed potatoes and some fresh-off-the-farm ears of corn. If you're looking to lighten up the meal a bit, you can serve these pork chops with lightly sautéed spinach.

1 Put the onion and half of the bacon crumbles in the slow cooker. In a small bowl, whisk together the broth, tamari, flour, garlic powder, thyme, and brown sugar. Pour the mixture into the slow cooker. Add the bay leaf.

2 Nestle the pork chops in the slow cooker. Lightly season the chops with salt and pepper.

3 Cover and cook on low for 4 hours.

4 Transfer the pork chops to a serving platter and tent loosely with aluminum foil to keep warm. Let them rest for 10 minutes.

5 Discard the bay leaf. Stir the vinegar into the sauce in the slow cooker. Spoon the sauce over the pork chops. Top with the remaining bacon crumbles and serve.

ALLERGY TIP If you are allergic to wheat flour, then you can use cornstarch or a gluten-free flour.

PER SERVING Calories: 516; Total Fat: 34g; Saturated Fat: 11g; Cholesterol: 86mg; Sodium: 852mg; Total Carbohydrates: 11g; Fiber: 1g; Protein: 46g

Cajun Pork Steaks

SERVES 4 • PREP TIME: 10 MINUTES
COOK TIME: 8 HOURS

BIG 8 ALLERGEN FREE
SET AND FORGET

**1½ pounds pork shoulder
steaks, trimmed of excess fat**

Salt

Freshly ground black pepper

1 cup barbecue sauce

1 teaspoon Cajun seasoning

½ teaspoon garlic powder

½ teaspoon onion powder

These pork steaks are perfect served with a fruit salad and a loaded baked potato. You can even cook the baked potatoes in the slow cooker at the same time as the pork. Just wrap the potatoes with aluminum foil and set in the slow cooker alongside the pork steaks.

1 Put the pork steaks in the slow cooker. Lightly season with salt and pepper.

2 In a small bowl, stir together the barbecue sauce, Cajun seasoning, garlic powder, and onion powder. Pour the mixture over the pork.

3 Cover and cook on low for 8 hours. Serve.

SIMPLE SWAP If you can't find pork steaks at your grocery store, you can substitute country-style pork ribs. Just trim off any excess fat.

PER SERVING Calories: 486; Total Fat: 32g; Saturated Fat: 11g; Cholesterol: 105mg; Sodium: 1,231mg; Total Carbohydrates: 23g; Fiber: 0g; Protein: 25g

Hoisin Pork Sliders

SERVES 6 • PREP TIME: 5 MINUTES
COOK TIME: 9 HOURS

SET AND FORGET

1 (2-pound) picnic pork roast, trimmed of excess fat

1 cup chicken broth

3 tablespoons hoisin sauce

2 tablespoons tamari or low-sodium soy sauce

1 teaspoon minced fresh ginger

1 teaspoon garlic powder

Hawaiian sweet rolls, for serving

Hoisin sauce is a thick, pungent sauce commonly used in Chinese cuisine as a glaze for meat, an addition to stir-fries, or a dipping sauce. The Asian flavors of this dish taste well paired with a sweet Hawaiian roll.

1 Cut the pork roast into four even pieces. Put the pork in the slow cooker. Pour the broth over the pork.

2 Cover and cook on low for 9 hours, or until the pork is fork-tender.

3 Transfer the pork to a cutting board and shred with two forks. Discard the broth in the slow cooker and return the pork to the slow cooker.

4 In a small bowl, whisk together the hoisin sauce, tamari, ginger, and garlic powder. Pour the sauce into the slow cooker and stir to coat the pork.

5 Cover and cook on high for 10 more minutes. Serve the shredded pork on Hawaiian sweet rolls.

ALLERGY TIP If you're allergic to wheat, serve your pork over hot cooked rice instead of rolls.

PER SERVING Calories: 417; Total Fat: 32g; Saturated Fat: 11g; Cholesterol: 107mg; Sodium: 692mg; Total Carbohydrates: 5g; Fiber: 0g; Protein: 27g

Country-Style Ribs

SERVES 6 • PREP TIME: 10 MINUTES
COOK TIME: 8 HOURS

SET AND FORGET

2 pounds boneless country-style pork ribs, trimmed of excess fat

¼ cup apple cider vinegar

¼ cup ketchup

1½ tablespoons brown sugar

1½ teaspoon chili powder

½ teaspoon smoked paprika

½ teaspoon ground cumin

½ teaspoon salt

¼ teaspoon freshly ground black pepper

Country-style ribs are nothing like a rack of ribs. They are slabs of pork that are sold either bone-in or boneless. These ribs cook all day long and taste divine served with a scoop of rice pilaf or mashed potatoes and a side of sautéed vegetables.

1 Put the ribs in the slow cooker.

2 In a small bowl, whisk together the vinegar, ketchup, brown sugar, chili powder, paprika, cumin, salt, and pepper. Pour the sauce over the ribs.

3 Cover and cook on low for 8 hours. Serve the ribs with the pan juices.

TASTY TIP To thicken the sauce and maximize the flavor, pour all the juices from the slow cooker into a saucepan and cook over medium heat for several minutes, stirring frequently.

PER SERVING Calories: 394; Total Fat: 29g; Saturated Fat: 9g; Cholesterol: 100mg; Sodium: 418mg; Total Carbohydrates: 8g; Fiber: 1g; Protein: 26g

Buffalo Pork Lettuce Wraps

SERVES 6 • PREP TIME: 5 MINUTES
COOK TIME: 8 HOURS

**BIG 8 ALLERGEN FREE
SET AND FORGET**

1 (2-pound) picnic pork roast, trimmed of excess fat

1 small yellow onion, quartered

1 cup chicken broth

½ cup buffalo sauce

6 large romaine lettuce leaves

This shredded pork is coated in buffalo sauce and then wrapped up in crisp lettuce leaves for an easy summer meal. Buffalo sauce is a combination of hot sauce mixed with melted butter. It's a toned-down, creamier version of hot sauce. It's still spicy, but not as intense. A little bit of buffalo sauce goes a long way.

1 Put the pork roast in the slow cooker. Nestle the onion quarters around the pork. Pour the broth over the pork.

2 Cover and cook on low for 8 hours.

3 Transfer the pork to a cutting board. Shred the pork with two forks. Discard the onion and liquid in the slow cooker. Return the meat to the slow cooker, pour in the buffalo sauce, and stir to combine. Place a heaping portion of pork on each romaine leaf and roll it up to eat.

PER SERVING Calories: 400; Total Fat: 31g; Saturated Fat: 11g; Cholesterol: 107mg; Sodium: 266mg; Total Carbohydrates: 2g; Fiber: 0g; Protein: 26g

Meat Sauce

SERVES 8 • PREP TIME: 10 MINUTES
COOK TIME: 8 HOURS

BIG 8 ALLERGEN FREE
SET AND FORGET

8 ounces lean ground beef

1 pound ground Italian pork sausage

1 (28-ounce) can crushed tomatoes

1 (14.5-ounce) can diced tomatoes
with green peppers, celery, and onions

2 tablespoons tomato paste

1 bay leaf

2 teaspoons dried basil

1 teaspoon garlic powder

1 teaspoon brown sugar

½ teaspoon dried oregano

Salt

Freshly ground black pepper

Italian sausage is the key to this delicious recipe. It gives the sauce so much flavor, the dish becomes a whole meal, especially when served with crusty bread and a side salad. You can choose a mild Italian sausage if you prefer less heat.

1 Combine the ground beef and ground Italian sausage in the slow cooker. Break up the meat with a wooden spoon. Add the crushed tomatoes, diced tomatoes with their juice, tomato paste, bay leaf, basil, garlic powder, brown sugar, and oregano. Stir well to combine.

2 Cover and cook on low for 8 hours.

3 Discard the bay leaf and stir. Season with salt and pepper and serve.

TASTY TIP To give this sauce even more depth and flavor, brown the beef and Italian sausage in a skillet before adding it into the slow cooker.

PER SERVING Calories: 295; Total Fat: 18g; Saturated Fat: 8g; Cholesterol: 59mg; Sodium: 816mg; Total Carbohydrates: 13g; Fiber: 4g; Protein: 20g

Lamb Steaks

SERVES 4 • PREP TIME: 10 MINUTES
COOK TIME: 5 HOURS

BIG 8 ALLERGEN FREE

3 garlic cloves, minced

¼ teaspoon salt, plus
more for seasoning

¼ teaspoon freshly ground black
pepper, plus more for seasoning

4 (4-ounce) boneless top round
lamb steaks, trimmed of excess fat

½ cup chicken broth

1 tablespoon chopped fresh basil

1 tablespoon chopped fresh mint

¼ cup chopped grape tomatoes

A lively relish of fresh basil, mint, and grape tomatoes tops these rich-tasting lamb steaks. Top round lamb steaks are a thick cut that is very tender. I like to serve these lamb steaks with roasted baby red potatoes and carrots or sautéed spinach.

1 In a small bowl, stir together the minced garlic, salt, and pepper. Rub the lamb steaks with the garlic mixture and put them in the slow cooker. Pour in the broth.

2 Cover and cook on low for 5 hours.

3 Transfer the lamb steaks to a serving platter. Season with additional salt and pepper. Top the lamb with a sprinkling of basil, mint, and tomatoes and serve.

SIMPLE SWAP Rather than mincing fresh garlic, you can buy a jar of minced garlic and keep it in your refrigerator. It would be handy for this recipe and many others.

PER SERVING Calories: 301; Total Fat: 24g; Saturated Fat: 10g; Cholesterol: 85mg; Sodium: 604mg; Total Carbohydrates: 3g; Fiber: 0g; Protein: 19g

Lamb Gyros

SERVES 6 • PREP TIME: 5 MINUTES
COOK TIME: 8 HOURS

SET AND FORGET

2 pounds lamb shoulder or leg chops

¼ cup fresh lemon juice

1 teaspoon garlic powder

1 teaspoon dried oregano

1 teaspoon salt

½ teaspoon freshly ground
black pepper

Pita bread, for serving

Chopped red onion, for serving

Tzatziki sauce, for serving

We love to serve our gyros with chopped lettuce and sliced tomatoes for a well-rounded meal. You can make your own tzatziki sauce (see page 64) or go the easier route and just buy a container of it at the store.

1 Put the lamb in the slow cooker.

2 In a small bowl, whisk together the lemon juice, garlic powder, oregano, salt, and pepper. Pour the mixture over the lamb.

3 Cover and cook on low for 8 hours.

4 Transfer the meat to a cutting board. Cut the meat into bite-size pieces and place on a platter. Serve each gyro with the lamb wrapped in pita and topped with chopped onion and tzatziki sauce.

ALLERGY TIP If you're allergic to dairy, serve the gyros without the tzatziki sauce. If you're allergic to wheat, serve the meat wrapped up in lettuce instead of pitas.

PER SERVING Calories: 441; Total Fat: 19g; Saturated Fat: 7g; Cholesterol: 150mg; Sodium: 906mg; Total Carbohydrates: 20g; Fiber: 2g; Protein: 47g

Lamb Shanks with Garden Vegetables

SERVES 4 • PREP TIME: 15 MINUTES
COOK TIME: 8 HOURS

2 cups frozen mirepoix

1 cup peeled, seeded, and chopped tomatoes

2 cups chicken broth

2 tablespoons tomato paste

1 teaspoon garlic powder

¼ teaspoon dried thyme

1 bay leaf

1 pound baby red potatoes, scrubbed

4 lamb shanks, trimmed of excess fat

Salt

Freshly ground black pepper

Braised in the slow cooker, these lamb shanks are extra tender and delicious. Smash the red potatoes and serve with the flavorful red sauce. And if you are hungry enough, the perfect accompaniment is a lightly dressed green salad.

1 Put the mirepoix, tomatoes, broth, tomato paste, garlic powder, and thyme in the slow cooker. Stir to combine. Add the bay leaf and potatoes.

2 Season the lamb shanks with salt and pepper. Nestle the lamb shanks in the slow cooker.

3 Cover and cook on low for 8 hours.

4 Discard the bay leaf. Transfer the lamb shanks and potatoes to a serving dish. Using an immersion blender, puree the liquid in the slow cooker until smooth. Pour some of the sauce over the lamb shanks and potatoes. Serve hot.

TASTY TIP To add depth of flavor, brown the lamb shanks before adding them to the slow cooker. Season the lamb with salt and pepper first, then heat 2 tablespoons of olive oil in a skillet over medium-high heat until it barely starts smoking. Add the shanks and brown on all sides.

PER SERVING Calories: 523; Total Fat: 20g; Saturated Fat: 7g; Cholesterol: 114mg; Sodium: 1,670mg; Total Carbohydrates: 42g; Fiber: 7g; Protein: 39g

10

SOMETHING SWEET

Peach Crisp

SERVES 5 • PREP TIME: 15 MINUTES
COOK TIME: 2 HOURS

3 large peaches, peeled, pitted, and sliced

⅓ cup all-purpose flour

⅓ cup quick-cooking oats

⅓ cup brown sugar

½ teaspoon ground cinnamon

⅛ teaspoon ground nutmeg

4 tablespoons (½ stick) unsalted butter

Vanilla ice cream, for serving

I love when fresh, fragrant peaches are in season. When they are cooked with this buttery oatmeal topping and topped with vanilla ice cream, it makes a perfect summer sweet treat. To prevent the topping from getting mushy, I place a double layer of paper towels on top of the slow cooker before I put on the lid. This prevents condensation from dripping down onto the peach crisp.

1 Put the peaches in the slow cooker.

2 In a medium bowl, combine the flour, oats, brown sugar, cinnamon, and nutmeg. Using a pastry blender, cut the butter into the flour mixture until it is crumbly. Sprinkle the mixture over the peaches.

3 Place a double layer of paper towels over the top of the slow cooker and then secure with the lid. Cook on high for 2 hours.

4 Serve with your favorite vanilla ice cream.

SIMPLE SWAP If fresh peaches aren't in season, you can use frozen peaches. You can find them in your grocer's frozen food section next to the berries. I don't like the way this recipe turns out when I use canned peaches, so try to use fresh or frozen.

ALLERGY TIP If you're allergic to wheat, you can use a gluten-free flour in the crumbles.

PER SERVING Calories: 207; Total Fat: 10g; Saturated Fat: 6g; Cholesterol: 24mg; Sodium: 69mg; Total Carbohydrates: 28g; Fiber: 2g; Protein: 3g

Banana Bread

SERVES 8 • PREP TIME: 15 MINUTES
COOK TIME: 2½ HOURS

⅓ cup milk

3 tablespoons canola oil

1 large egg, lightly beaten

3 medium ripe bananas, mashed

2½ cups all-purpose flour

½ cup granulated sugar

½ cup brown sugar

3½ teaspoons baking powder

1 teaspoon salt

Banana bread is a classic, but it bakes for a long time, and with my duties, I sometimes need some wiggle room with the baking time. When cooking in the slow cooker, the bread will be fine if I need to leave for a few minutes to pick up a child from an activity. It's not going to burn as it would in the oven. I also like to make banana bread in the slow cooker in the hot summer months because I don't have to turn on the oven.

1 In a large bowl, whisk together the milk, oil, egg, and mashed bananas. Add the flour, granulated sugar, brown sugar, baking powder, and salt. Stir until just combined and no flour streaks remain.

2 Grease a loaf pan that will fit inside your slow cooker insert. Pour the batter into the loaf pan.

3 Place a trivet in the bottom of your slow cooker. Place the loaf pan on the trivet. Place a double layer of paper towels on top of the slow cooker and secure with the lid. Cook on high for 2½ hours.

4 Remove the loaf pan from the slow cooker and let it sit for 15 minutes. Slice and serve warm.

INGREDIENT TIP Whenever I have a bunch of brown bananas, I peel them and put them in a resealable plastic freezer bag. Then when I need some for banana bread or a smoothie, I have them on hand.

ALLERGY TIP If you're allergic to wheat, use a gluten-free flour. If you're allergic to dairy, use unsweetened almond milk in the place of regular milk. If you're allergic to eggs, use an egg replacer.

PER SERVING Calories: 333; Total Fat: 7g; Saturated Fat: 1g; Cholesterol: 24mg; Sodium: 317mg; Total Carbohydrates: 66g; Fiber: 2g; Protein: 6g

Dulce de Leche

SERVES 8 • PREP TIME: 5 MINUTES
COOK TIME: 4 TO 8 HOURS

1 (14-ounce) can sweetened condensed milk

Milk (optional)

This caramelly sauce is perfect to dip Granny Smith apples into or to serve over ice cream.

1 Remove the paper label from the can of sweetened condensed milk. Place the unopened can on its side in the slow cooker. Fill the slow cooker with water until it is 1 to 2 inches above the height of the can.

2 Cover and cook on high for 4 hours or on low for 8 hours.

3 Turn off the slow cooker and carefully remove the unopened can with a pair of tongs. Place it in the refrigerator and chill until ready to serve. Open the can and stir with a spoon. If needed, you can thin the caramel with a little bit of milk. Add 1 tablespoon of milk at a time and stir until it gets to the desired consistency.

INGREDIENT TIP If you'd rather, you can cook the caramel in mason jars. You'll need three 4-ounce jelly jars. Open the can of sweetened condensed milk and divide it between the jars. Seal the jars and place them in the slow cooker, then add the water. You'll be able to tell what color the caramel sauce is since the jars are transparent. The longer you cook it, the darker the color will become. These make nice gifts, along with a few Granny Smith apples.

PER SERVING Calories: 159; Total Fat: 4g; Saturated Fat: 3g; Cholesterol: 17mg; Sodium: 63mg; Total Carbohydrates: 27g; Fiber: 0g; Protein: 4g

Chocolate Fondue

SERVES 6 • PREP TIME: 5 MINUTES
COOK TIME: 30 MINUTES

6 ounces semisweet chocolate

½ cup heavy cream

Suggested dipping treats: pretzels,
banana slices, angel food cake squares,
strawberries, graham crackers,
marshmallows, dried pineapple rounds

Who doesn't like dipping food in chocolate? You can
get really creative with all the dipping treats. Just go
to the grocery store and get inspired.

1 Break up the chocolate into small pieces and put them
in the slow cooker. Pour the cream over the chocolate.

2 Cover and cook on high for 30 minutes. Stir. If melted,
then turn the slow cooker to warm. If it's not melted, then
cook on high for a few more minutes until it is. Dip your
favorite treats in the chocolate.

SIMPLE SWAP I prefer semisweet or dark chocolate, but if you're a
milk chocolate lover, you can use high-quality milk chocolate chips
in this recipe.

PER SERVING Calories: 48; Total Fat: 4g; Saturated Fat: 3g;
Cholesterol: 14mg; Sodium: 5mg; Total Carbohydrates: 2g;
Fiber: 0g; Protein: 0g

Hot Chocolate

SERVES 10 TO 12 • PREP TIME: 5 MINUTES
COOK TIME: 1 TO 1½ HOURS

8 cups milk

1 (14-ounce) can sweetened
condensed milk

2 cups semisweet chocolate chips

1½ teaspoons vanilla extract

1 teaspoon salt

This is a super rich and indulgent treat. I love to make hot chocolate in the slow cooker for holiday parties because it stays warm and ready to serve at all times.

1 Combine the milk, sweetened condensed milk, chocolate chips, vanilla, and salt in the slow cooker and stir.

2 Cover and cook on high for 1 hour. Whisk. If the chocolate is melted, it's ready to serve. If not, cover and cook for another 30 minutes and check again.

3 Turn the slow cooker to warm. Serve the hot chocolate in mugs.

SIMPLE SWAP   You can use dark chocolate chips in place of the semisweet chips. I wouldn't use milk chocolate in this recipe, because with the sweetened condensed milk the hot chocolate would be too sweet.

PER SERVING Calories: 287; Total Fat: 10g; Saturated Fat: 6g; Cholesterol: 34mg; Sodium: 395mg; Total Carbohydrates: 41g; Fiber: 0g; Protein: 11g

Chocolate-Covered Nut Clusters

MAKES 18 • PREP TIME: 5 MINUTES
COOK TIME: 1 TO 2 HOURS

1 (16-ounce) package chocolate
or vanilla-flavored candy
coating (almond bark)

1 (16-ounce) jar salted
dry-roasted peanuts

These chocolate-covered nuts are a fun holiday treat. The recipe makes a lot, so it's perfect to share at a party or to give away to friends.

1 Put the candy coating in the slow cooker.

2 Cover and cook on low for 1 hour. Stir. If needed, cook for another hour and stir again.

3 Stir the peanuts into the chocolate until coated. Use a spoon or a scoop to drop the peanut-chocolate mixture onto parchment paper. Allow to set completely for 1 hour before serving.

SIMPLE SWAP You can use a different type of nut if you prefer. Or you can use a variety of nuts like pecans, macadamias, almonds, and walnuts.

PER SERVING (1 cluster) Calories: 274; Total Fat: 20g; Saturated Fat: 6g; Cholesterol: 5mg; Sodium: 226mg; Total Carbohydrates: 19g; Fiber: 2g; Protein: 7g

THE DIRTY DOZEN AND THE CLEAN FIFTEEN

A nonprofit and environmental watchdog organization called Environmental Working Group (EWG) looks at data supplied by the US Department of Agriculture (USDA) and the Food and Drug Administration (FDA) about pesticide residues and compiles a list each year of the best and worst pesticide loads found in commercial crops. You can refer to the Dirty Dozen list to know which fruits and vegetables you should always buy organic. The Clean Fifteen list lets you know which produce is considered safe enough when grown conventionally to allow you to skip the organics. This does not mean that the Clean Fifteen produce is pesticide-free, though, so wash these fruits and vegetables thoroughly.

These lists change every year, so make sure you look up the most recent before you fill your shopping cart. You'll find the most recent lists as well as a guide to pesticides in produce at EWG.org/FoodNews.

2017 Dirty Dozen

Apples	Strawberries
Celery	Sweet bell peppers
Cherry tomatoes	
Cucumbers	In addition to the Dirty Dozen, the EWG added two foods contaminated with highly toxic organophosphate insecticides:
Grapes	
Nectarines	
Peaches	
Potatoes	
Snap peas	Hot peppers
Spinach	Kale/Collard greens

2017 Clean Fifteen

Asparagus	Mangoes
Avocados	Onions
Cabbage	Papayas
Cantaloupe	Pineapples
Cauliflower	Sweet corn
Eggplant	Sweet peas (frozen)
Grapefruit	Sweet potatoes
Kiwis	

MEASUREMENT CONVERSIONS

Volume Equivalents (Dry)

US STANDARD	METRIC (APPROXIMATE)
⅛ teaspoon	0.5 mL
¼ teaspoon	1 mL
½ teaspoon	2 mL
¾ teaspoon	4 mL
1 teaspoon	5 mL
1 tablespoon	15 mL
¼ cup	59 mL
⅓ cup	79 mL
½ cup	118 mL
⅔ cup	156 mL
¾ cup	177 mL
1 cup	235 mL
2 cups or 1 pint	475 mL
3 cups	700 mL
4 cups or 1 quart	1 L
½ gallon	2 L
1 gallon	4 L

Volume Equivalents (Liquid)

US STANDARD	US STANDARD (OUNCES)	METRIC (APPROXIMATE)
2 tablespoons	1 fl. oz.	30 mL
¼ cup	2 fl. oz.	60 mL
½ cup	4 fl. oz.	120 mL
1 cup	8 fl. oz.	240 mL
1½ cups	12 fl. oz.	355 mL
2 cups or 1 pint	16 fl. oz.	475 mL
4 cups or 1 quart	32 fl. oz.	1 L
1 gallon	128 fl. oz.	4 L

Oven Temperatures

FAHRENHEIT (F)	CELSIUS (C) (APPROXIMATE)
250°F	120°C
300°F	150°C
325°F	165°C
350°F	180°C
375°F	190°C
400°F	200°C
425°F	220°C
450°F	230°C

Weight Equivalents

US STANDARD	METRIC (APPROXIMATE)
½ ounce	15 g
1 ounce	30 g
2 ounces	60 g
4 ounces	115 g
8 ounces	225 g
12 ounces	340 g
16 ounces or 1 pound	455 g

RECIPE INDEX

INDEX

ACKNOWLEDGMENTS

Many thanks to the many friends and family members who helped me so much during the recipe testing process of my cookbook! Namely Jaymee Sire, Suzanne Stratton, Natalie Bentley, Barb Woodward, Elizabeth Weiler, Cathy Jeppsen, Gina Benson, Nicole Gamble, Mikelle Kostial, Sabrina Schuler, Brittney Boyle, LuAnn Bellessa, Brittney Bellessa, Misty Hope, Nancy Leavitt, Melissa King, Kristen Hills, Trulee Goble, Alicia Unruh, Janaya Rampton, and Emily Nelson. I couldn't have done it without you. My family also deserves acknowledgment because they had to live with me when I was slightly stressed out for a bit. I appreciate their constant support and encouragement. I'm also very appreciative of all the help from the fabulous people at Callisto Media.

ABOUT THE AUTHOR

Karen Bellessa Petersen is a food blogger and cookbook author. She started her blog, 365DaysOfCrockPot.com, in 2009 and has been creating scrumptious slow cooker meals ever since. Besides making easy meals in her slow cooker, she also enjoys spending time in the kitchen baking cookies. (Karen lives and breathes cookies, and will eat them at every opportunity she can—she's made it her mission to make sure people never have to settle for mediocre desserts!)

Because she makes (and eats) so much food, Karen exercises regularly to maintain balance in her life and spends a lot of her free time running and hiking. She loves to compete against herself and improve her health and performance. A devout churchgoer, Karen also delights in studying the scriptures and is a huge fan of podcasts, which she'll listen to any chance she gets.

Karen lives near Salt Lake City with her handsome husband, Greg, and their two amazing children, Reagan and Skyler. She loves watching her children participate in sports and other activities, and she dreams of the day when they learn to love running as much as she does.

CPSIA information can be obtained
at www.ICGtesting.com
Printed in the USA
BVOW11s1000250817
492912BV00007B/15/P